POLITICS OF SPACE AND THE QUESTION OF PALESTINE

POLITICS OF SPACE AND THE QUESTION OF PALESTINE

SHAKEEL ANJUM

ADROIT

Adroit Publishers

NEW DELHI • KATHMANDU

ISBN : 978-81-87393-56-6

2018

Published by
ADROIT PUBLISHERS 4675/21, Ganpati Bhawan, Ansari Road,
Daryaganj, New Delhi-110 002 Phone : 011-23266030
adroitpublishers@gmail.com
C/O Vajra books, Thamel, Jyatha,
Kathmandu, Nepal l KTM: +977-9808357451

Jacket Design—Sukruti Anah Stanley

Cover Photograph—Bassam Almohor

Typeset in Garamond Premier Pro by Arun, Akriti Graphic Solution, Delhi-110081 E-mail: arun263923@gmail.com, Ph: 9999414390

For Elizabeth Philip, A.K Ramakrishnan &
M.H. Ilias
Friends, Teachers, Critics

CONTENTS

Acknowledgements

These aching memories of knowing are so many debts of lines, truths, terrains, trains, traces, memories, love, friendship and trails of thought to the depository of names one has gathered in the dust that life is. These names are so many places of love, encounters, and friendships, truths- damp, bitter, dry and sweet. These names are precisely debts, non-refundable, but returnable to a certain degree by recalling the memory of encounters that these names are. One by one, I must return to these names as a promise of my own return to the idea of friendship: Professor M.H Ilias, Nawang, Asif K.V., Sukrita Lahiri, Ashutosh, Sukriti Anah Stanley, Gautam Buddha Rai, Ghulam Mustafa, Elizabeth Philip, Mahmoud Al-Zayed and my family.

There are hardly any teachers left and I am very lucky to find one whom I can address as my teacher, my master (in the craftsmanship sense) and my guide: Professor A.K. Ramakrishnan. He is not a teacher, rather so many fragmented lines of a broken mirror into which one's one face is indiscernible without there being the idea of a mirror at first place. This book is born of the Master's of Philosophy dissertation weaved under his constant gaze, a gaze so soft and tender, yet so piercing that words, sentences, points, marks yield to his soft handling of philosophical scalpel. It is to him that I am indebted for unraveling the mysteries of fiction, autobiography and truth bound in flesh and metaphor.

Perhaps I would never be able to utter a name dipped in love, passion and heart. There is anxiety and nervousness not because I am not able to call her name here, but anxiety is precisely there because of the weight that her gesture carries. Between these words, in silences, and around lies a void without which we would be unable to decipher the words, precisely. Like words, and winter she multiplies the void around me and these voids are so many fragmented spaces of solitary journey towards love. Her presence and absence around me, her walking into the maze of this book's so many drafts, lines, commas, exclamation marks, dashes, full stops, citations, references, etc. has made this work possible. Between words, walking through the maze of these voids and coldness of winter, I wish to return to her, through these words, without the sound of name.

Finally, I also wish to acknowledge my debt to Professor K.M Seethi, editor of *Indian Journal of Politics and International Relations* for publishing my essay, Geo-*Graphical* Conditions: Memory, Time, and Rift in Vol. 9, No. 1, 2016. The revised version of the published essay is being presented to the dear reader as one of the chapters in the book.

Foreword

The stones from most Palestinian hills are fast disappearing. The smaller ones are picked up by the Palestinian children to frighten the Israeli tanks. Their source for the sustenance of struggle is draining out as very many hills have become monstrous settlements of the colonizer. The everyday realities of Zionist colonialism have been redrawing Palestinian landmaps and lifemaps to such extent that mooring oneself in one's own land becomes difficult. This uprooting of the lifeworld of Palestinians and the disorientation that results from it can only be addressed through memory. The deep connection between land and memory is what Palestinians establish both in the actualities of the shrinking space in their everyday lives and in the imaginative geographies of freedom and independence. The sense of loss and discontinuities of territorial flow inflicted by the past and contemporary colonial occupation compel Palestinians to search for that organic connection with the contiguous land which can only be captured now with a sense of belonging in a struggle that continuously imagines and reimagines a peoples' collectivity. In this sense, for Palestinians spatiality is collectivity in thought and actions that rejoins a fractured land.

Palestinians in exile hold on to memory of the lost and ever losing land and they listen to the call of the land to return, however difficult that may sound now. The 'exilic displacement' that Edward Said talks about in fury and lamentation is somewhat reconciled by him by treating 'out of place' as a habit and place of habitation. In his poem *Counterpoint* written as a farewell to Said, Mahmoud Darwish writes:

My exile is the backdrop of epic scene,
I defend the poet's need
to join tomorrow with memories,
I defend trees the birds wear
as country and exile.
I defend a moon still fit for a poem of love.
I defend an idea fractured by its owner's fragility
And a land the myths have kidnapped.

These lines of defense that Darwish tightly holds to are not merely those associated with trenches and accords, but those integrally connected to the human imagination and creativity. Darwish wants to 'invent a hope for words/ or an area or a mirage to prolong hope./ And sing, for beauty is freedom.'

Raja Shehadeh's multiple walks through the Palestinian landscape by appreciating the variety of plants, the smell of flowers and the soil, the gardens, the olive trees (that live forever) and the beauty of the hillocks, are not only an attempt to create an aesthetic map of Palestinian lifeworld, but also a retrieval and accumulation of the aesthetic and political resources for a struggle. There has been an investment of memory in space both by Israelis and the Palestinians. As often described, the crux of the Palestinian-Israeli conflict is the contending claims of two nationalisms directed towards the same land. What is important to note is the question of power in the claims of the same land and the actualities of the change induced in that piece of land. The ongoing Zionist colonization of Palestinian land through ever-expanding settlements in the West Bank and the military occupation of the Palestinian territories are integral parts of that power imbalance. Everyday colonial expansion is redrawing the physical and the mental map of Palestine. For the Palestinians to have a livable land —and we need to recognize that to have a life worth living, it has to happen in an intimate space, a familiar space where one feels a sense of belonging—the world of memory, the temporal world has to nest in a spatial world that sustains life and is one that is worth struggling for. The spatial imagination in itself contains layers of temporality. If contemporary capitalist globalization heralds the triumph of time by annihilating space, the Palestinian imagination of space has rich and diverse imaginations of time and memory. The memories here make the space worth longing for. For Palestinians, spatiality in itself becomes the centre of political contestation and struggle.

Shakeel Anjum has drawn from a variety of sources to make us aware of the significance of land and memory in Palestinian lives. He has creatively interwoven memories and desires to draw a 'cartography of becoming'. Self, self-determination, sovereignty and freedom are the subterranean currents in Anjum's aesthetico-political imagination of Palestinian lives. I am immensely happy to partake in his labour of writing this book, and for me, this is a labour of love.

A.K. RAMAKRISHNAN

Preface

Here is a map of our country:
Here is the sea of indifference, glazed with salt
This is the haunted river flowing from brow to groin.
This is the desert where missiles are planted like corns
[...] This is the cemetery of the Poor
Who died for democracy
[...] I promised to show you a map you say but this is a mural
Then yes let it be, these are small distinctions
Where do we see it from is the question.

—Adrienne Rich, An Atlas of the Difficult World

The history of nineteenth century European colonialism is the history of continued expansion and domination of the territories by subjugating the natives, disciplining them, and ruling over them, controlling them and also dominating and erasing cultural spaces of the natives. It is in this context we must see the two grand hegemonic ideas of the 19th century, European colonialism and Zionism. Palestine has been key to colonial domination for the British and French imperial imagination. Palestine has been imagined and promised as national home for the Jewish diaspora by the French under Napoleon Bonaparte in his failed attempt to capture Acre in 1799 as it is claimed by some Zionist historians (Schechter 2003, Millgram 1990). Palestine was envisioned and promised as a national home for the Jewish diaspora by another colonial power, Great Britain which successfully helped the Zionists in colonizing Palestine and declaring the statehood of

Israel in 1948. Since then, the question of Palestine and the fate of the Palestinians living in exile or in continuous occupation by Israel has remained a key issue in world politics.

How does discourse on the linearity and homogeneity 'on/of/about' (Lefebvre 1991) space affect individuals, cultures and societies? Is the question of Palestine only a tussle between two national imaginations in which both the Israeli and the Palestinian narratives are intertwined in a historical battle of claims and counterclaims? Is it not a question of geography where space is treated as 'the dead, the fixed, the undialectical, the immobile' against the notion of time full of 'richness, fecundity, life, dialectic' (Foucault: 1980)? What are the consequences of imagining the colonized geographies as a battle of the narratives in the linearity of history?

The colonial and the Zionist narratives have imagined Palestine as an 'empty' space and as a 'land without people for a people without land'. The geographical imagination of Palestine as an 'empty' space and 'making the desert bloom' obscured the reality of the history and geography of Palestine inhabited by Palestinians. It's in the same light that Palestine was envisioned as a 'national home' for the Jewish diaspora in the first Zionist Congress held in Basel, Switzerland in 1897 under the leadership of Theodore Herzl. The Zionists from there on tried to lobby different colonial powers, presenting the map of Palestine as their future homeland. The reimagination of Palestine was received by Great Britain with enthusiasm. In 1917, Lord Balfour, British Foreign Secretary, in a private letter to a prominent Jewish businessman, Lord Rothschild promised 'the establishment in Palestine of a national home for the Jewish people'. The League of Nations put the administration of the territory of Trans-Jordan and Palestine under the British mandate in 1922. Britain facilitated the immigration of Jews to Palestine, provided institutional, material and the ideological support to the Zionists to buy lands from the Palestinian absentee landlords which swelled to a total of 5.5 percent of the land by 1948. The moment Britain left Palestine, the Zionists proclaimed independence in 1948. Since then the state of Israel has been continuously dispossessing the Palestinians out of their territory in an effort to seek Grand Israel, thereby marginalizing the Palestinian spaces.

The imagination of the space out there to be captured, dominated through a process of 'ethnic cleansing' (Pappé 2006) led to the creation of the state of Israel in 1948. The question of Palestine is a contestation of 'imaginative geography' and the material practices through which the reality of geography has been altered. It's a contestation between mental invention of people as a nation and the real people inhabiting that space. The experiences of the Palestinians living in forced exile or as second class citizens inside Israel are real and lived experiences of the social life of the space, as opposed to the imagined, invented mental spaces for the Israelis. Many of the present generation of the Palestinians are tied to their ancestors who had lived and experienced the place while on the other hand, many of the present generation of Israelis are descendants of the wave of the migration from various parts of the world who had set their foot for the first time in Palestine. The colonial power has played an important role in obscuring the real history and geography of Palestine.

What does the al-Nakba mean for the Palestinians who have been erased from their land, their villages pillaged, evacuated forcefully, and turned into a state of permanent exile? How do we really come to terms with politics, memories and the reality of the Palestinian lives, their culture and landscapes which have been completely transformed by the Israeli occupation? What does it mean when a Palestinian living in exile on the periphery of Palestine still holds the key of his/her house from where he/she was forcefully evicted? Palestinians exiled still hope of returning to their native land in future. What are the ways in which spatial narratives of the Palestinians are constructed? That is why mapping Palestine and its cultural landscape from the account of those exiled and their writings about spaces from where they were forced into exile becomes an important tool for enquiry into the nature of occupation. Challenging the Zionist architecture of erasures is a crucial task from the standpoint of those who were forced into exile.

The 'geographical imagination' of space in terms of its appeal to the mythical past and the capitalist 'accumulation by dispossession' (Harvey 2003) go hand in hand. Since 1967, combined with a force of biblical fantasies and modern machinery, the goal of the Israeli state is to occupy maximum land minus the Palestinian people while at the same time crippling the Palestinian economy. The control of land, resources, and utilizing the Palestinian workforce which strengthens the Israeli economy is a key to the occupation of the Palestinian territory. The creation of 'apartheid wall', building checkpoints, denial of access to Palestinian territories, building separate roads for settlers, are examples which undermine the political and economic freedom of the Palestinians. The Israeli state continues to dispossess Palestinians by economic blockades on occupied territories. There is an important link between maintaining the Jewish identity, culture and politics on one hand, and the political economy on the other. The uneven development of the Palestinian occupied territory is a result of Israel's diversion of important resources to the Jewish settlements in occupied Palestine.

The imaginative geography and the colonization by accumulating more spaces and resources for the grand idea of constructing an *Eretz* Israel has led to the loss of land, livelihood, dignity and economic strangulation for the people living under Israeli settler-colonial domination. The continued building of illegal settlements by the Israeli state, building of separation wall, checkpoints, the policies of spatial segregation, dividing people within the occupied spaces and appropriating labour power are the patterns of spatial practices. The spaces lived and experienced by the Palestinians manifested in a number of ways, including the textual and oral narratives are being transformed into a zone of exclusion by the Zionist architecture of erasures to deny the Palestinians their right to return and live with dignity.

The question of Palestine is largely imagined and portrayed as common sense objectivity in the realm of world history as 'Israel-Palestine conflict' over a territory. The same common sense objectivity of history obscures the political and the colonial imagination behind the occupation of a geographical region. This brings us to the dominance of historical time over that of space, a geographical category. The role of 'imaginative geography' as Edward Said (1993) put it or 'geographical imagination' and 'accumulation of capital by dispossession' as David Harvey (1990 & 2003) suggests, becomes an important factor in the discourse of Palestine. It is very important to question the role of the power of the imagined as 'imaginative geography' which obscures the lived reality of spaces, its stories and plays a crucial role in defining the present state of affairs. The architecture of renaming and refashioning of places to suit national and hegemonic interests according to the 'invented tradition' as Eric Hobsbawm suggests, is an attempt to erase the history of the spaces lived and experienced by the actual inhabitants. How do the spatial practices dominate the social life and culture of that specific space? How are images about certain places or spaces created? What are the sources of power that are involved in providing a meaning to certain ideas of a particular space into reality?

The understanding of space thus becomes an important tool for understanding the relations between empire, power, and capital. Lefebvre (1991) argues how spaces are produced by human actions through three different domains of lived experiences (material practices), perception (representations of space) and imagined or conceived (representational spaces). Harvey (1990: 218-222) expands Lefebvre's (1991) thesis on three aspects of space into different spatial grids. In lived experience (material practices), spaces are produced by design of physical infrastructures, building network of communications, transport, and territorial organizations. In the domain of the perceived (representations of space), space is produced via maps, visual representation, discourses on architecture, language, etc. and in the realm of conceived or imagined spaces (spaces of representation), spaces are produced as a result of utopian ideas, imaginary landscapes, novels or fiction, poetics of space, spaces of desire, etc. The work attempts to look at the ideology of Zionism as spatial practice in its entire avatar in the light of Lefebvre and Harvey's conceptual grid of spatiality.

'The construction of new dominant mental conceptions and material practices with respect to space and time', as Harvey suggests, 'were fundamental to the rise of capitalism.' There is an important link between the 'cultural politics and political economic power which plays an important role in social construction of place' Harvey (1996: 238). The construction of place according to the homogenous imagery 'of beliefs, values, ideals and persuasions with a strong sense of collective memory and spatial exclusionary rights', Harvey suggests, 'can be extraordinary players on the world stage' (ibid.: 323).

Edward Said (1992: 57) views that the Zionism as an ideology can be understood 'genealogically' and as a 'practical system of accumulation'. Conceptions of space as 'empty' and 'inhabitable' do not exist in the world and we cannot imagine ourselves without 'geography' and the 'struggle over geography' (Said 1993: 6). While referring to the French philosopher Gaston Bachelard, Said argues that the poetic meaning of space which has 'imaginative' power overrides the objective qualities of space (Said 1995: 54-55). A space can be 'haunted, or homelike or prisonlike or magical'. The poetic process of space gives it an emotional and rational content. The identity of the 'other' and the spaces they occupy become the source of the imaginative geography and the representations of other cultures beyond 'our' territory become fictitious. Said's analysis of Zionism as a politico-spatio-literary practice which has gained legitimacy in the Western world and its representation in the works of prominent literary figures like Jane Austen, Moses Hess, a prominent Zionist ideologue, and Theodore Herzl etc., underlines how Zionism has been perceived, imagined, constructed, and actualized on the ground by the assistance of major European powers.

Is the space a homogenous entity which stands still where time moves into past, present, future in all possible directions, roams freely and comes back to settle on space? Is space not a dimension of multiplicity? Is there a single story of space or there are 'stories', 'trajectories', 'coevalness' as Massey (2005) suggests? What are the consequences of going back into space and time? Can we really go back into space and time without anticipating any backlash? Doesn't space throw up? These are some of the important questions on the discourses on/of/about about space that Massey (2005) provides a clue in order to understand the complexities of space in relation to the question of *othering*. The understanding of space 'conceived as something malleable and usable is a prerequisite to the domination and control of the space through human action', suggests Harvey (1990:254). It is this concept that led these figures to imagine Palestine as 'empty' territory and 'a land without people for a people without land'. Those who 'command spaces, writes Harvey, 'also controls the politics of that space'. The continued domination and occupation of Palestine by the Israeli state is an example of the command of space and control of the politics of Palestine in neo-colonial times with multiple consequences. How is the question of ideology linked to the question of space? 'What is an ideology without a space', asks Lefebvre (1991: 44). A spatial enquiry is required to understand the politics of ideologies like Zionism and the questions of nationhood linked with spatial practices by the Israeli state. At the same time we would have to look at different ways of spatial resistances in 'contrapuntality', to use Edward Said's word, a point missing in Henri Lefebvre and David Harvey's idea of spatiality. Palestinians so far have been engaging in multiple ways and methods of resisting the spatial practices of the Israeli 'colonial-settler state': imaginatively by creating an inventory of writing and as well as through acts of bodily resistances— *sumud.*

The first chapter deals with the linkages and connections between imperialism and Zionism. The imperialist and Zionist conceptions of space and time have been detrimental not only to the Palestinians but to Arab Jews as well and Zionism's failure to understand the complexities of construction of a homogenous space has led to a condition where Israel as a nation state is haunted both from within and without. A nation state based on exclusive Jewish identity has produced a class of refugees, crises and ruptures within the Jewish state of Israel. The writing of Amos Oz, a prominent literary figure has been taken up for looking at the concept of spatial imagination of Zionism and the question of *other.* Oz's autobiography is central to understanding the current crisis of the Jewish state. The chapter moves on to discuss how Zionism is understood from the point of view of the Palestinians and the Arab Jews and the inherent crisis within the psyche of the Israeli state and its people. This chapter begins with the problematique of the spatio-temporal relations and major concepts and discourses on the question of space, time and literary imaginations concerning Palestine. Space is key to understanding power relations and its operation in cultures and societies of the modern times.

The Second and Third Chapters consecutively deal with the memoirs of Raja Shehadeh and Mourid Barghouti. In their memoirs Shehadeh and Barghouti capture the loss of the Palestinian culture and the landscape. Through their writings Shehadeh and Barghouti create a narrative of dispossession, exile and estrangement (both internal and external). Palestinian resistance through the concept of repetition, deterritorialization of the hegemonic narratives of Zionism and resistance by way of writing is to produce an inventory of narratives challenging the Zionist imaginations of space.

The fourth chapter deals with the questions of imaginative geographies along with the political economy of imperialism and Zionism. Zionism as an ideology is engaged in spatial practices by a combination two forces: brutal 'accumulation by dispossession' and violent 'geographical imagination', simultaneously. This chapter explores how the flawed understanding of spaces on the basis of the Jewish exclusive rights based on religion and Biblical imagination (raw colonialism in the guise of messianic home place) coupled with materialistic aims of state has continued to colonize and dominate the Palestinians until now.

ONE

ISRAEL AS FICTION, PALESTINE AS DOCUMENTARY

Just as none of us is outside or beyond geography, none of us is completely free from the struggle over geography. That struggle is complex and interesting because it is not only about soldiers and canons but also about ideas, about forms, about images and imaginings.

— *Edward W. Said*

There would appear to be a landscape whenever the mind is transported from one sensible matter to another, but retains the sensorial organisation appropriate to the first, or at least a memory of it. The earth seen from the moon for a terrestrial. The countryside for the townsman; the city for the farmer. Estrangement would appear to be a precondition for landscape.

— *Jean F. Lyotard*

Reading Space-Time-Body Relations in Israel/Palestine

Given the layers of contradictions in political, nationalist, cultural and academic discourses in relation to spatial-temporal dichotomy of Israel/Palestine, any definition of space-time relations has to reach conclusive ideas only after reading *histories* against history and *geographies* against geography. The geography of Israel/Palestine as a territory is a palimpsest of histories, stories, memories and displacements. Therefore one has to acknowledge multiple dimensions of space-time relations against the claim of one hegemonic discourse. The claim of a linear trajectory of history and story over a place by a group or nation denies the *histories* and *stories* of others over the same territory. Henri Lefebvre and David Harvey argue that space-time is a social and historical construct. If people make their histories then Edward Soja (1989) would argue that people make their geographies too. Marx writes in his *The Eighteenth Brumaire of Louis Bonaparte,* 'all facts and personages of great importance in world history occur, as it were twice: the first time as tragedy, the second as farce' (Marx 1977: 10). Marx was half correct, geography also repeats, first as a tragedy, second as a farce. In the imagination of a nation state like Israel, time has to freeze; it has to come to a halt in order to conceive a space of the biblical imagination. Israel's quest for 'redeeming the land' for its Jewish diaspora by a combination of 'intelligence and stupidity', to use Mourid Barghouti's term, has led to a farce not only in terms of history but in terms of geography as well. The Israel/Palestine question poses a definitional problem in situating itself within the discourse of the post-colonial. Locating Israel among the league of post-colonial nations will deny the Palestinians their history, memory and geography. The problem is posed by Joseph Massad (2006) eloquently in his work *The Persistence of the Palestinian Question: Essays on Zionism and the Palestinians*. The paradox he points out here is that the pre-1948 temporal structure from Israel's point of view is a colonial time dominated by Arabs in which the Jewish people were the ones who were colonized. And yet, given the history of Israel as settler-colonial project of imperialism since 1948, Palestine becomes a colonized geography in which Palestinians and Arabs become subjects of Israel. Also the location of Arab Jews in the Israeli/Palestinian context puts them in a conflicting position— as colonizer and the colonized. Massad locates Palestine as the 'post-colonial' colony because of the complex relations between time and space.

> The synchronic presentation of the Zionist project as colonial and anti-colonial coupled with the diachronic process of transforming its explicitly colonial heritage as anti-colonial shows the palimpsestic nature of current Zionist historiography. Moreover, the dual status of Mizrahi Jews as colonizer and colonized renders the national space and time within and during which they live as colonial/postcolonial synchronically. What is then this space and time called Israel? What constitutes the difficulty in naming it in relation to colonialism? Can one determine the coloniality of Palestine/Israel without noting its "post-coloniality" for Ashkenazi Jews? Can one determine the postcoloniality of Palestine/Israel without noting its coloniality for Palestinians? Can one determine both or either without noting the simultaneous colonizer/colonized status of Mizrahi Jews? How can all these people inhabit a colonial/postcolonial space in a world that declares itself living in a post-colonial time? (ibid.: 14)

Oren Yiftachel, a Post-Zionist geographer develops a geographical critique of hegemonic nationalist theories by Gellner, Hobsbawm *et al.* by calling it '*spatial blindness*', for confusing state-building with nation-building that led these theoreticians 'often privileging the dynamics of *time* over *space*' (Yiftachel 2002: 220-221). In Yiftachel's view, the Israel/Palestine question is rather geographical than it is historical. 'The Palestinian *Nakba* and Jewish *Shoah* became deeply etched in the collective memories of the two national movements' by aspiring to '*enter history through territory*' (ibid.: 227). Yiftachel, unlike other Post-Zionists agrees with the Palestinian narrative that Zionism evolved as a colonial project. 'Time–space interactions', as Yiftachel argues, 'became crucial for Zionism. It was embodied in the perception that resurrecting Jewish history is only possible in the Land of Israel' (ibid.: 224). 'National time' was brought in to justify a colonial project, 'in effect, a-historical, providing a unified, linear and repeatedly recited backdrop for contemporary practices of territorial expansion' (ibid.: 224). Since the beginning, 'space, place and territory became the kernels of the Zionist project' (ibid.: 224). Yiftachel terms Israel as an 'ethnocratic state' where 'exclusive ethno-national culture was coded, institutionalized and militarized by the new state, in order to quickly 'indigenize' immigrant Jews, and to conceal, trivialize, or marginalize the land's Palestinian past' (ibid.: 228).

Derek Gregory in his analysis of the present situation in Iraq, Afghanistan and Palestine contests the idea of the prefix 'post' in postcolonial studies. Taking cue from Walter Benjamin's idea of history, Louis Althusser's critique of temporality and Akhil Gupta's critique of the postcolonial condition, Gregory argues that if temporalities are heterogeneous then one cannot really cut a cross-section through multiplicities of social change. The 'capacities that inhere within the colonial past are routinely reaffirmed and reactivated in the colonial present' (Gregory 2004: 7). There is a break from the past as postcolonial critics would argue but Gregory's assumptions about the present condition are apt as imperialism has the power to intervene in our daily lives. The 'war on terror' provided a justification, a cover for the U.S. invasion of Iraq and Afghanistan and Israel's colonial control over Palestine. These acts on behalf of power testify to the fact that colonialism did not break from its past but appears in a new avatar which continues in the 'present tense' (ibid.).

Within the geographical boundaries of Israel/Palestine bodies can be seen in conflict, jostling to claim a space of their own, denied by the colonizing practices of Israel. Israel's continued colonization of Palestine, denial of rights of the Palestinians to their state and its rough treatment to Mizrahi or Arab Jews are manifestations of discriminatory spatial practices inherent in colonialism. Ideology is linked to space and 'achieves its consistency by intervening in social space and its production, and by thus taking on body therein. Ideology *per se* might well be said to consist primarily in a discourse upon social space' (Lefebvre 1991: 44). Conflicts over geography or geopolitical conflicts always use 'aestheticization of politics' through a process of imagination of the past in terms of mythology of place (Harvey 1990: 209). In the case of Israel the 'aestheticization of politics' by Zionism has resulted in the most reactionary of colonial practices creating a system of apartheid in Palestine. Drawing an understanding from the works of Lefebvre, Harvey and others it can be argued that the organization of social space is really important in defining the nature of a state. The contradictions in spatial practices of Israel are revealed by the process of its historical and cultural productions, narratives, stories, memoirs, etc. The contradictions, tensions, nightmares, revulsion, fear, which appear especially in its literary and cultural productions, are a manifestation of Israel's spatial practices of colonization, domination, segregation and other forms of control. In *A Thousand Plateaus* written in 1980 by Gilles Deleuze and Félix Guattari, geography is 'not only physical and human but mental as well, like the landscape' (Dosse 2010: 254). If we take Deleuze and Guattari's idea of 'territorialization' then Zionism as an ideology in the beginning, de-territorialized Palestine by the sheer force of arms resulting in 'ethnic cleansing' and destruction of the cultural, political and physical landscape; then re-territorialized it along the idea of the exclusive 'Jewish state'. Deleuze and Guattari further extended the idea of 're/de-territorialization' in *Anti-Oedipus,* and *Kafka: Toward a Minor Literature* which is based on a geo-philosophical study of Kafka's works. To bring the idea of 're/de-territorialization' in a generic sense of the term in the case of literary productions within the geographical boundaries of Israel, it can be adduced that the majority of literary productions are the repetition of dominant Israeli narratives, with few exceptions which try to 'de-territorialize' the Zionist imagination by breaking the boundaries and thereby exposing Zionism. To buy Deleuze and Guattari's arguments, there is a 're-territorialization' at work in the works of fictions or memoirs which strengthens the logic of colonial expansion and subjugation of the Palestinians in writings that are produced within Israel. Deleuze himself was sympathetic towards the cause of the Palestinians. In an interview with Elias Sanbar, Deleuze compared the history of Israel with the history of America where the native people were wiped out from their native geographies (Deleuze et al. 1998).

Amos Oz and the Fiction of Zionism

Amos Oz is a prominent Israeli novelist whose literary works have travelled beyond Israel and have been translated into many languages. His autobiography appeared at the height of *Intifada* and in a political milieu in which other suppressed identities within Israel were vying for a political and social space. The publication of his autobiography was followed by a series of reviews in leading journals and newspapers both within and outside Israel, especially in the western press and academia which as a rule is a blocked terrain for the Palestinian narratives (Rose 1996; Bugeja 2012). In *A Tale of Love and Darkness,* Oz delves into nostalgia and produces a memory of his family life that migrated from Eastern Europe to Palestine in the early 1930s. Oz narrates his childhood, the lives of his mother and father paralleled with the developments in the Mandated Palestine leading to the creation of the State of Israel. He traces the life of the Klausner family (father's side) in Odessa and Vilna and the Mussman family (mother's side) in Rovno, a small town in Western Ukraine. The Klausner family was a hardcore supporter of right wing politics and an admirer of the Jabotinsky brand of Zionism. Oz later considered himself to be a 'Beginite' till he switched sides and went to work in Kibbutz Hulda. Central to his autobiography is his mother Fania, who commits suicide in her sister's apartment in Tel Aviv at the age of thirty-eight when Oz was just twelve years old. Interestingly, what we see and observe in *A Tale of Love and Darkness* is a story about his mother and her turbulent relationship with the new space that is Israel with which she is unable to co-opt and reconcile her Eastern European past while Amos Oz's Jerusalemite childhood and his growing fondness for the new state ready to be born, successfully reconciles with the politics of Zionism and the nationalism which claims Palestine as a homeland for Jews. What we see in *A Tale of Love and Darkness* is a play of contradictions in which bodies diverge and travel in opposite directions in a single geographical terrain, a contestation and tussle between two distinct imaginations and visions; one diasporic, exilic and the other nationalist. The final outcome of the tussle is a victory of the Zionist and nationalist vision over the diasporic, exilic vision. Oz's depiction and construction of his childhood memory, his father's life and the development of Zionism revolves around the life of his mother Fania which acts as the negative of a film from where he creates a positive image in the form of the grand narrative of a nation. Throughout his novel he portrays women, Arabs and other Jewish identities in photographical negativity so as to develop a grand and singular narrative structure of muscular Zionism.

Zionism and its Other Within: Othering the Mother

Guarded by well-armed soldiers.
Again the need of establishing a new identity
To fit a new homeland is made clear:
I paid five shillings and changed my ancestral name
From the diaspora to a proud Hebrew name to match hers.

— Yehuda Amichai, *The Great Tranquility* (Bugeja 2012)

A Tale of Love and Darkness is a narrative spanning over 500 pages in which Fania Mussman appears as a central character. Oz's language in his autobiography reads like a fictive language where the difference between a novel, a work of fiction and autobiography is blurred or there is a very thin line which separates an autobiography from fiction (Negev 2011).[1] Amos Oz throughout his career, as Eran Kaplan

1. Negev writes that there is a similarity of narratives in his Novel, *Fima* and his autobiography, *A Tale of Love and Darkness* where after his mother's death the apartment where Amos lived with his family in Jerusalem became very chaotic and

(2007) writes, 'exemplified the Zionist quest to create a universal subject and to condense the past—the national as well as personal—to its purest form.' Since childhood Oz was fascinated with war and strategies of regaining the 'homeland'. He would collect 'paperclips, a pencil sharpener, a couple of small notebooks, a long-necked inkwell full of ink, a rubber, a packet of drawing pins, and use all these to construct a new frontier kibbutz', to defend itself from 'a gang of blood-thirsty marauders' and finally would defeat his enemies by opening 'fire and with a few furious salvoes they will wipe the trapped enemy force, chanting hymns of glory...' (Oz 2004: 29). He turned his home - toys, tables, chairs, sofas, etc. as a battleground for strategies. The autobiography is further full of games of his childhood where he sees himself as a soldier, or a pioneer defending the 'homeland'. It is a sign of how the whole Israeli society is militarized to such an extent that a child takes to thinking in terms of military moves and strategies; this was during the 1940s when Zionists were arming and training themselves with the aid of imperial power later to result in the 'ethnic cleansing' of Palestine. Unconsciously, the culture of militarization was absorbed by a child.

The performative aspects of Zionism as a cultural phenomenon in literary reportage veiled as fiction can be seen broadly at work in Oz's narrative of his childhood. Here the function of memory, that of childhood, engaged in geopolitical maneuvers is not an independent one but the very idea of memory being harnessed to attain certain political ends of a culture. Balibar and Macherey (1996: 61) argue,

---

littered for several weeks. Negev writes, 'Oz scattered other pieces of himself in other novels. When I asked him about the resemblance between him and Fima of "The Third Condition" (published in English in 1993 as "Fima"), a man who lives in filth and unbelievable disorder, and dreams of advising the government and repairing Israeli society— Oz responded angrily, 'Don't confuse my underwear with my characters' underwear.' I felt like a snoop, and wondered whether I was the 'panting interviewer,' as Oz put it in a later book, the interviewer who attempts to disassemble the skeleton and remain with the bones.'

'the objectivity of the literary production therefore is inseparable from the given social practices in a given Ideological State Apparatus. The production of literature is not separated from its society and culture but is a product of the dominant ideology'. Balibar and Macherey (ibid.: 61) further write, 'literature is historically constituted in *the bourgeois epoch* as an ensemble of language—or rather of specific linguistic practices—inserted in a general schooling process so as to provide appropriate fictional effects, thereby reproducing bourgeois ideology as the dominant ideology' (ibid.: 61). Zionism as an idea and as the 'settler colonial' project unleashed its own brand of fictions and narratives which blocked other narratives from raising their voices. The Klausner family was an ardent supporter of Right wing revisionist Zionism led by Jabotinsky. Arieh Klausner, father of Amos can be seen in the autobiography narrating the poems of Jabotinsky. In an interview Oz (1996a) responds to a question about the authors who had made a lasting impression on him:

> When I was nine or ten, I read Zionist books about the glories of the ancient kingdoms of Israel. I decided to become a *terrorist* against the British Mandate; I built an intercontinental rocket with the wreck of a refrigerator and the relic of a motorcycle. My plan was to aim this rocket at Buckingham Palace, then send a letter to the King of England saying, Either you get out of my country or off you go! I was an intifada child against the British—I threw stones at British soldiers and shouted, Go home. So my early reading was nationalistic [Emphasis added] (Oz 1996a).

The use of the word 'terrorist' by Amos Oz has never been questioned or put under a critical scrutiny in this interview whereas the Palestinians are always bombed with similar clichés. Their acts of resistance are always questioned by the West so as to put the Palestinians under the disciplinary regime of language in international politics which invariably favours Israel.

As Karen Grumberg (2010) argues, 'though Oz devotes far more space to his father's frustrated intellectual ambitions, it is his mother whose character and spirit animates his thoughts, musings, and recollections throughout the six hundred pages.' Oz further gives a description of his parents as:

> Both my parents had come to Jerusalem straight from the nineteenth century. My father had grown up on a concentrated diet of operatic, nationalistic, battle thirsty romanticism (the Springtime of Nations, *Sturm und Drang*), whose marzipan peaks were sprinkled, like a splash of champagne, with the virile frenzy of Nietzsche. My mother on the other hand, lived by the other romantic canon, the introspective, melancholy menu of loneliness in a minor key, soaked in the suffering of broken hearted, soulful outcasts infused with vague autumnal scents of *fin de siècle* decadence (Oz 2004: 241).

Oz's narrative of his mother as 'melancholy' and 'soulful outcast' is in sharp collision with that of his father who is portrayed as a 'nationalistic and battle thirsty romantic'. His mother's image is portrayed as the negative of a film connoting something dark from which father's vision of nationalism comes out. Oz writes further,

> My mother lived a solitary life, shut up at home for the most of her time. My mother found no interest in Jerusalem... The Zionist fervor of those who built new suburbs, who purchased and cultivated virgin lands and paved roads, while it intoxicated my father to some extent, passed my mother by (ibid.: 262-263).

While Oz was fascinated and lost in 'the smell of the land from time immemorial', Fania had no interest in Zionism. For her there was 'no gate' and she considered Zionism as an 'abyss' (ibid.: 324). For Oz the 'Zionist enterprise was born out of monumental visions' (Oz 1996: 106). For most of her life after arriving in Palestine in 1934, Fania remained a solitary figure in the Klausner family of intellectuals which passionately discussed politics of everyday life and the future of Zionism. Oz writes about his mother:

> My mother's stories were strange: they were nothing like the stories that were told in other homes at that time, or the stories I told my own children, but were veiled in a kind of mist, as though they did not begin at the beginning or end but emerged from the undergrowth, appeared for a while, arousing alienation or pangs of fear moved in front of me for a few moments like distorted shadows on the wall, amazed me, sometimes sent shivers up my spine, and slunk back to the forest they had come from before I knew what had happened (Oz 2004: 132)

Oz remarks that he spent most of his childhood 'on the edge of the forest, by the huts, the steppes, the meadows' that filled his mother's basket of stories and he felt that he was in the east but his heart 'was in the farthermost west or the farthermost north' (ibid.: 134). Fania 'maintained the dark winters of Europe in the very fiber of her being, a state that contributed to her gradual withdrawal from life in Palestine' (Grumberg 2010: 378).

Oz's writings 'depict two elements, two principles of existence: on the one hand there is a feminine element, symbolized by the ocean, the ring, darkness and the unconscious; on the other hand, there is the masculine element symbolized by land, a straight line, light, consciousness' (Balaban 1990: 81). Balaban writes further that the 'dual structure of conflict and conciliation' allows Oz to frame a grand narrative and merge the 'battling forces into a single unitary existence' (ibid.: 88). There are not only two principal elements of contradiction which allow Oz to form a grand narrative; there are other elements as well, the 'blood thirsty' Palestinians and Arabs, the 'suntanned Jews' in a list of other *others* which constitute the making of a single grand narrative much like the convergence of different notes in a musical composition, only to cast away the darkness and the silence, essential elements which provide meaning to a melody.

In an interview in 2004 Amos Oz remarked about his mother's suicide:

> She died because for her, Jerusalem was an exile. This climate and environment and reality was alien. And she died because her hopes, if she had any, that maybe a replica of her Europe could be built here, without the bad aspects of the diaspora Jewish shtetl, were apparently refuted by the reality of the morning after (Kaplan 2007: 140).

After his mother's death Oz rebelled against the conformist ideas of his parents which subscribed to far right ideology of the Jabotinsky and later, Menachem Begin. He was carried away by the idea of Kibbutz life. Oz writes,

> After a year or two, when I'd left home and gone to live in Kibbutz Hulda, I slowly started to think about her, too... I would sit there in the dark for half an hour or an hour, conjuring up, picture by picture, the end of her life. In those days I was already trying to imagine a little of what had never been spoken about, either between my mother and me, or between me and my father, or apparently even between the two of them... My mother was thirty eight when she died... Ten or twenty years after they completed their studies at the Tarbuth secondary school, when my mother, Lilenka Kalisch, and some of their friends experienced the buffeting of reality in a Jerusalem of heatwaves, poverty and malicious gossip, when those emotional Rovno schoolgirls found themselves in the rough terrain of everyday life, napkins, husbands, migraines, queues, smells of mothballs and kitchen sinks, it transpired apparently that the curriculum of the school in Rovno in the twenties was of no help to them. It only made

> things worse... Perhaps something of the childhood promise was already infected by a kind of poisonous, romantic crust that associated the muses with death? (Oz 2004: 205-209)

Amos Oz abandoned the Klausner title and changed his name to Amos Oz, Oz meaning "might". He was to live in Kibbutz from 1954-1985. Oz writes further:

> The death of all the grown-ups concealed a mysterious, powerful spell. And so at the age of fourteen and a half, a couple of years after my mother's death, I killed my father and the whole of Jerusalem, changed my name, and went on to Kibbutz Hulda to live there over the ruins (ibid.: 445).

Oz remarks that the 'suffocation of life in that basement' with his parents and between the ambition of his father and mother's 'nostalgia for Rovno... embodied by a black tea-trolley and gleaming white napkins, the burden of his failure in life, the wound of hers' oppressed Oz so much that he wanted to 'run away from it' (ibid.: 414). Oz was inspired by Tsi Livne's book *Over the Ruins* which portrays a deep hatred and contempt for the older generation. He writes:

> There may be well another sick illicit pleasure concealed here, one that no doubt never occurred to Tsi Livne when he was writing the book, a dark Oedipal pleasure. Because the children here buried their own parents. All of them. Not a single grown up was left in the entire village. No parents, no teachers, no neighbor... And so a well repressed desire of the Zionist ethos, and of the child I was then, was miraculously fulfilled: that they should be dead. Because they were so alien, so burdensome. They belonged to the Diaspora. They were the generation of wilderness... Only when they are dead will we be able to show them that at last we can do everything ourselves.... Because the new Hebrew nation needs to break free from them (ibid.: 445).

Eran Kaplan notes, at a juncture in Israeli history when other identities were vying for a political space, 'Oz tells the story not of a hegemonic Zionist group but rather of one group among many others that compete in an ever-expanding cultural arena' and 'the Zionist ideal of the negation of the past is replaced by an attempt to recover a (personal as well as collective) traumatic past' (Kaplan 2007: 140). 'The space that homogenizes', as Henri Lefebvre argues, 'has nothing homogenous about it. After its fashion, which is polyscopic and plural, it subsumes and unites scattered fragments or elements by force' (Lefebvre 1991: 308). Zionism here becomes the homogenizing force where colliding identities are brought together to form one homogenous identity and transform it into nationalism. Oz beautifully transcends from his past through the image in which Fania emerges as the dominant figure. It is through Fania, a metaphor of dark, melancholy, sad figure that Oz depicts as the negative of the film from which a positive image of Zionism and the birth of a new nation emerges. As Norbert Bugeja observes, 'ultimately it is Fania – in a replication of the historical endorsement of Jewish ostracism and ghettoization in Europe who has to "fade away" in order for the nation to be born' (Bugeja 2012: 98).

Zionism and its Other Other: 'Bloodthirsty' Arabs

> *Conquest of the earth, which mostly means taking it away from those who have a slightly different complexion or slightly flatter noses than ourselves, is not a pretty thing when you look into it too much.*
>
> —Joseph Conrad, Heart of Darkness

As Marlow in Joseph Conrad's *Heart of Darkness* is fascinated with maps and would find himself lost in the glories of exploration, Amos Oz's autobiography is full of fascination with empty spaces, land, arms, uniforms, battleships and so on. *A Tale of Love and Darkness* is full of racist vocabulary portraying the Arabs in an essentialist frame. Despite many critical works by historians, critics challenging the official historiography by Zionist revisionist scholars, Oz in his autobiography speaks in the same language and tone as is used by the British and Zionist colonizers, administrators, literary figures right from the nineteenth century. As Edward Said puts it, 'Zionism essentially saw Palestine as the European imperialist did, as an empty territory paradoxically "filled" with ignoble or perhaps even dispensable natives' (Said 1992: 81). Oz's writing too is filled with such 'guttural shrieks' (Oz 2004: 610).

Theodore Herzl had the same view on the idea of a Jewish state. He held that the Jewish state would be

> a rampart of Europe against Asia, an outpost of *civilization* as opposed to *barbarism*. We should as a neutral State remain in contact with all Europe [Emphasis added] (Herzl 1989:13).

Further down the line Oz describes about the landscape of Palestine in the same vein as described by early Zionist leaders from Herzl to Chaim Weizmann. Weizman describes the landscape of Palestine as 'rocks, marshes and sand, so that its beauty can only be brought out by those who love it and will devote their lives to healing its wounds' (Said 1992: 85). Oz draws an imaginary map of Palestine as 'hot, a wilderness, swamps' full of unemployed people and he goes on to describe the population and states that 'there weren't many Arabs, there may have been less than one million'. It was an established fact that there was a space and that space was filled with people. At first, as Said argues, Zionists tried to 'minimize, then to eliminate and then, all else failing, finally to subjugate the natives' (ibid.: 84). Just like Marlow in *The Heart of Darkness*, the whole world for Oz seemed to be an 'empty space' as Oz as a child imagined with his

> handful of toothpicks, a couple of bars and soaps, three toothbrushes and a half-squeezed tube of Ivory toothpaste, plus a hairbrush, five of Mother's hairpins, Father's toilet bag, the bathroom stool, an aspirin packet, some sticky plasters, and a roll of toilet paper were enough to last me for a whole day of wars, travels, mammoth construction projects and grand adventures in the course of which I was, by turns, His Highness, His Highness's slave, a hunter, the hunted, the accused, a fortune-teller, a judge, a seafarer, and an engineer digging the Panama and Suez canals through difficult hilly terrain to join up all the seas and lakes in the tiny bathroom and to launch on voyages from one end of the world to the other merchant ships, submarines, warships, pirate corsairs, whalers and boatloads of explorers who would discover continents and islands where no man had ever set foot (Oz 2004: 250).

Oz is full of contempt for the Arabs and his first encounter with an Arab family led to a tragic episode. Eran Kaplan comments on this encounter as a result of 'some primordial, instinctive, tribal hatred between the Jewish and Arab children' and 'the very nature of differences made them fight each other' (Kaplan 2007:134). The very portrayal of this encounter as 'primordial, instinctive and tribal' obscures the fact that 'in Jewish hearts, however, Israel had always been there, an actuality difficult for the natives to perceive' and 'Zionism therefore reclaimed, redeemed, repeated replanted, realized Palestine, and the Jewish hegemony over it' (Said 1992: 87). The idea of how another could inhabit a space which was always there in waiting for the wandering Jewish diaspora to inhabit got carried into a child who thinks of the Arab in terms of an outsider in orientalist vocabulary. It is not unnatural for a child to consume a discourse already hegemonized in Jewish culture that the space was always 'empty' and consequently, theirs to take over.

During the course of the visit to the Silvani family in Sheikh Jarrah in East Jerusalem, Oz as a child is invited by another child, Aisha to climb up a tree and Oz takes up the challenge and was 'excited and perhaps a little in love with her and yet trembling with the thrill of national representativity, eager to do anything she wanted, I instantly transformed myself from Jabotinsky into Tarzan' (Oz 2004:315). After climbing up the tree Oz whirls the iron chain with a feeling of 'muscular Judaism taking the stage, the resplendent new Hebrew youth at the height of his powers, making everyone who sees him tremble at his roar: like a lion among lions'. In the process Awwad, Aisha's brother is hurt and Oz portrays Aisha's reaction which still runs into the memory. Oz writes, 'But I do remember to this day, like two sharp burning coals her eyes beneath the mourning-border of her black eyebrows that joined in the middle: loathing, despair, horror and flashing hatred came from her eyes... you could sniff it from a long distance away. Like a bad smell' (ibid.: 317). Aisha with a metaphor of darkness, horror, and full of hatred is an Arab, the other. As Bugeja observes, the description of Aisha 'represents Oz's principal engagement with some form of Palestinian consciousness' (Bugeja 2012: 109) and the 'Arab's operative function is both limited to and constituted by her designation as an aggressive agent who threatens the tranquillity of the narrator's perspective. For Oz Aisha represented a citizen of 'other Jerusalem', which Oz portrayed in his essay titled, 'Alien City'. The 'other Jerusalem' as Oz writes, 'the one surrounding my city, which sent alien, guttural sounds rippling towards us and smells, and flickering pale lights at night, and the frightening wail of the muezzin towards the dawn' (Oz 1996:178). In the midst of the violence, Oz recalls Aisha in his memory. Oz writes,

> And how about Aisha and her parents in Talbieh? Was her whole family sitting in a room full of men with moustaches and jewelled women with angry faces and eyebrows that met above their noses, gathered in a circle around bowls of sugared

> orange peel, whispering among themselves and planning to 'drown us in blood'? Did Aisha still sometimes play tunes she had learnt from her Jewish piano teacher? Or she was forbidden to? (Oz 2004: 336)

And further,

> Where did Aisha go, with her little brother? To Nablus? Damascus? London? Or to the refugee camp at Deheisha? Today if she is still alive, Aisha is a woman of sixty five. And her little brother, whose foot I may have smashed, would be nearly sixty now (ibid.: 355).

As Bugeja argues, Aisha in the memory of Oz is confined to 'an obscure existential vacuum' away from a landscape in some refugee camps from where Israel as a nation emerges. Two contradictory elements occur in Oz's narrative about Aisha. On the one hand, Aisha is an Arab seeking revenge while on the other hand, there is a rupture in Oz's own narrative which moves in the other direction, that of identification of a shared culture of cohabitation where Aisha's piano teacher is of Jewish origin. In the unconscious part of Oz's imagination there is a history of coexistence, of cohabitation of Arab-Jewish culture. The existence of Judeo-Islamic culture is blurred to frame a nationalist narrative and the formation of the *other*—the other that is constitutive of the *self* is erased objectively to serve ideological functions whereas subjectivity retains the *other* as fragments of a vessel in the unconscious. In the introduction of his essays under the title, *Under This Blazing Light*, Oz writes that 'the case between Israelis and the Palestinians is a tragedy precisely because it is a clash between one very powerful claim and another' (Oz 1996: 5). Bugeja further observes that reading Oz's statement in the light of representation of the Palestinians in *A Tale of Love and Darkness,* 'what seems to beg urgent revision in that statement is the sheer scale of an asymmetry in the representation of the two claims that in Oz's account, remains largely unaccounted for' (Bugeja 2012: 110). In his autobiography Oz denies the fact that the space was inhabited by the Palestinians and they too have a claim on that space. Oz carries the same version as of Zionist historiography which portrays the Arabs as aggressors and denies al-Nakba and the violent expulsion of Palestinians from their own space. Oz has reversed his statement of 'right versus right' in his autobiography and expelled the other right. He wrote, 'we were in the goodies, we were right, we were innocent victims.' (Oz 2004: 322).

Oz has dramatically minimized the catastrophe in the making of the nation of Israel. The fact is that 1948 saw what Ilan Pappé (2006) calls 'the ethnic cleansing of Palestine', resulting in the violent, architectural expulsion of the Palestinians known as al-Nakba was consistently denied by official Zionist historiography was later exposed by 'New Historians'. Between September 1947 and March 1948, 70,000 Palestinians were forced to leave their homes and this exodus 'produced a collective sense of insecurity and terror among the many segments of the Palestinian urban population' (Bugeja 2012: 109).

Oz comes out with a detailed narrative of events from the UN Partition voting up to the creation of the state of Israel. What is surprising is that despite the challenges to the official narrative of Israel from the New Historians group after their reading of the Israeli archives in the 1980s, Oz still clings to the same narratives portraying Arabs as aggressors and the Jews as 'alone and defenceless in the sea of Arabs' (Oz 2004: 330). Oz recalls the events on the eve of UNSCOP resolution which divided Palestine into two unequal halves. Oz writes,

> The areas allocated to the two states were *almost equal in size*. The complicated, winding border that separated them was drawn roughly in accordance with the *demographic distribution of the respective populations*. The two states would be linked by a common economy, currency, etc. Jerusalem, the committee recommended, should be neutral

> *corpus separatum,* under the international trusteeship with a governor appointed by the UN.
>
> These recommendations were submitted to the General Assembly for its approval, which required a two-thirds majority. The Jews gritted their teeth and *agreed to accept* the partition proposal: the territory allocated to them did not include Jerusalem or upper and Western Galilee, and three quarters of the proposed Jewish state was *uncultivated desert land.* Meanwhile the Palestinian Arab leadership and all the nations of the Arab league declared at once that they would not accept any compromise, and that they intended to resist by force the implementation of these proposals, and to drown in blood any attempt to create a Zionist entity on the single inch of Palestinian soil [Emphasis added] (ibid.: 323).

This shows how Oz has internalized the official Zionist narrative, continues with the one which has been contested by the New Historians. As Bugeja notes,

> Oz's endorsement of the Israeli national historians' narrative, with its effective sanitization of the true upheaval that changed the face of Palestine is not, of course, the last word on the matter. What is difficult to come to terms with about his account is that the memoirist- a self confessed laborite peace activist- penned *A Tale* some fifteen years after the emergence of the New Historians in Israel. Benny Morris, Ilan Pappé, Avi Shlaim, Tom Segev, and others have long been contesting the conventional version of the events as the establishment had propagated hitherto (Bugeja 2012: 111).

Oz goes on to say that the division of Palestine by the UN Resolution 181 was *equal* and in tune with the *demographic distribution of the respective populations.* Given the facts and the history produced by the New Historians, Oz is factually wrong. Ilan Pappé writes that by the end of the mandate in 1947, the Jews were holding ownership over only 5.8 percent of the land and almost all the cultivated land in Palestine was held by the Palestinian population (Pappé 2006: 30). Pappé further notes, 'the UN totally ignored the ethnic composition of the country's population. Had the UN decided to make the territory the Jews had settled in Palestine correspond with the size of their future state, they would have entitled them to not more than ten per cent of the land' (ibid.: 34). The Jews owning less than six per cent of the land and a population around one third of Palestine were handed more than 50 per cent of the land. Was it not unjust? Let us have a look at the demographic composition of the distribution of land. Palestine's division into three parts would have given 42 per cent of the land to the Palestinians in which 818,000 Palestinians would make a state comprising 10,000 Jews, while the Jewish state with almost 56 per cent of the land would comprise 438,000 Palestinians (ibid.: 35). Pappé goes on to say, 'had the Arabs or the Palestinians decided to go along the Partition Resolution, the Jewish leadership would have been sure to reject the map the UNSCOP offered them' (ibid.: 35). Yes, the Palestinians rejected the Partition Plan from the very beginning as it was undemocratic and nowhere in the world would any native population have ever accepted the Partition of their territory as against their own wishes and shared the territory with a settler colonial project.

The Zionists agreed to the Partition Plan but with a tactical purpose. Pappé argues that once it was clear that the Palestinians were in complete rejection of the Partition Plan, it was easy for Ben-Gurion and his team to accept it but partially. Pappé writes, 'the delineation of final borders would remain an open question', and Ben-Gurion, 'as unhappy as he was with the UN map... what mattered was international recognition of the right of the Jews to have a state. . .' (ibid.: 36).

It has now become an established fact that there was a complete Plan by the Zionists for an 'ethnic cleansing of Palestine' and there was a complete asymmetry of power, military might, ideological support and logistics between the Palestinians and the Zionists and despite all this, Oz provides a narrative which reflects the entirety of the politics of victimhood. Oz writes that as the British would leave, 'hordes of bloodthirsty Arabs, millions of fanatical Muslims, would be bound to butcher the whole lot of us in a few days. They would not leave a single child alive' (Oz 2004: 288). Oz further reverses the whole process of the 'ethnic cleansing' and writes that it was the Arabs who implemented 'a more complete "ethnic cleansing" in the territories they conquered than the Jews did: hundreds of thousands of Arabs fled or were driven out of the territory of the state of Israel in that war, but a hundred thousand remained, whereas there were no Jews, at all in the West Bank or the Gaza Strip under Jordanian and Egyptian rule' (ibid.: 328). Oz is completely in tune with the official narrative of the Israeli victimhood which continues to this day. He is in complete denial of the catastrophe which Palestinians call al-Nakba. For Oz, 'war was a terrible thing of course...' but who asked the Arabs to start it? (ibid.: 370). As Bugeja observes, 'Oz does not attempt to contextualize that aggression historically; neither does he feel the political imperative to explain the processes that led to it. He certainly does not attempt any empathetic representation of the conflict from the Palestinian viewpoint. There is no reference whatsoever to Israel's cleansing of 370 Palestinian villages (on some accounts by historians the number of villages erased is more than 400) and three quarters of a million Palestinian Arabs who became refugees as a direct consequence of Israel's establishment—almost 90 per cent of those living in the territories designated by the UN as a Jewish state' (Bugeja 2012: 113). In fact, there was a much more brutal plan of the ethnic cleansing by the Zionist army known as Plan Dalet or simply Plan D. The plan was exercised to perfection in three phases as Ilan Pappé observes. Oz's collusion with the official Zionist history and its claim that the Palestinians were not forced to leave but they were asked by their Arab leaders to do so, actually serves the Zionist purpose. Oz himself acts as an apologist for the whole Zionist politics of undermining the truth and denying space to the Palestinian voices. His autobiography as Bugeja observes is a turning back to his efforts at the Oslo peace process 'as a dialectical activity in an incessant pursuit of alternative political and historical answers to the predicament of Israel-Palestine' (ibid.: 114). Just after the Oslo peace process, there was a sharp increase in the building of illegal settlements by the Israeli administration coupled with the building of a massive apartheid wall. Israel's continued strangulation of the Palestinian economy, a direct control of Palestinian political, social and economic life through checkpoints, building separate roads much like Bantustans in apartheid South Africa has resulted in a process of total blockade. Israel has been the beneficiary of the peace process and Oz himself commented after the Oslo peace process that it is the 'second biggest victory of Zionism' (Bove 2000: 28).

What emerges in *A Tale of Love and Darkness* is an apologia for Zionist colonization. Oz's memoir repeats his 1968 novel, *My Michael,* where Hannah Gonen, the heroine of the novel feels herself to be a 'conqueror' and the two Palestinian Arab boys are her 'native bearers'. As Jacqueline Rose (2008) observes, 'Oz therefore allows the young girl to act out the reality of colonial power between Jew and Arab even during the mandate period before Israel was born'. Oz himself will never acknowledge that Israel is a colonial power as Rose argues, but his character in the novel, *My Michael* acts a 'trope'. Rose is of the opinion that Oz would not repeat the same endeavour again in his writings 'today, when suicide attacks have given to this vision an abhorrent reality,' but his memoir, just as Rose suggests by laying open the cadaver of *My Michael,* repeats the character again this time not in the cloak of a feminine body but of himself as an actor. *A Tale of Love and Darkness* is a memoir of colonial fantasies par excellence. Israel's colonial subjects are not only Palestinians but Arab Jews as well. Arab

Jews do not find a space in Oz's entire memoir except as 'suntanned Jews' who must disappear in the project of 'Eretz Israel' as a domain and exclusivity of Ashkenazi dominance.

Zionism from the Standpoint of its Two Victims: Palestinians and the Arab Jews

In his collection of essays, *The Discourse on Colonialism* which was first published in 1950, Aimé Césaire exposes the politics and culture of the 'civilizing' mission of the European civilization. Césaire develops a critique of modernity, similar to Theodore Adorno's critique of enlightenment where the cultural roots of fascism and colonialism could be located within the project of enlightenment itself. For Césaire, European civilization's claims to a superior culture based on race and means of production, its claim of bringing 'civilization' to the 'uncivilized' races and the cultures of nations across Asia, Africa and Latin America renders unacknowledged the brutality in its own genesis. The same Europe which underprivileges, dominates and inferiorizes the other has displayed in its history, the worst form of butchery, racism and barbarism. Césaire here is talking about Nazism which 'oozes, seeps, and trickles down from every crack' of the European civilization (Césaire 2010: 36). The imperialist practice of colonialism in its various forms has exposed itself on the ground that the principal idea of holding on to the native land of Asians, Africans and Latin Americans, its culture and its civilization was an idea based on a relationship of master-slave authorized by the elemental discovery of science by the West. The politics of civilization continues to this day albeit in other forms. Civilization has been replaced by the word 'democracy' and its master craftsmen are the Americans who until recently have been engaged in teaching the lessons of democracy, prominently in Iraq, Afghanistan, Syria and Yemen primarily through bombings, torture, drone warfare and other forms of brutality.

In the context of Palestine, the Zionist practice of land confiscations by eliminating the Palestinians from their own space and culture through various means of subjugation, architectural segregation, exploitation of resources and labour both via institutionalized processes of the state and para-state entities in the form of settler violence and racism in recent times has led to the condemnation by a prominent Israeli writer as actions equivalent to neo-Nazism. On 10th May, 2014, Israeli Daily *Haaretz* reported Israeli right-wing vandalism and racism against the Christian minorities in Israel. On the walls of a church in Jerusalem, graffiti reads, 'King David is for the Jews, Jesus is garbage'. The writing on the wall clearly suggests how racism has become a dominant part of Israeli cultural common sense, not to mention the daily acts of suffering inflicted on the other minorities within Israel—the Palestinians and the Arab Jews. This act of vandalism was condemned by Amos Oz. He referred to right wing groups as the 'Hebrew Neo-Nazis'. In Oz's view, acts of violence and racism like these tarnish the image of Israel in the international public opinion, so it must be condemned but he does not reflect on the brutality meted out to Palestinians, Christians and Arab Jews in totality by the state machinery of Israel. Moreover, Zionist project of building a 'homeland', and the architectural facade that Zionism is, is built on the very ideas of modernity and enlightenment and Oz fails to reflect on its racial foundations of brutality and exclusion.

Zionism as a 'settler colonial state' and as a product of European colonialism as Edward Said puts it, has been detrimental to the Palestinians as it has forced them to live as exiles and refugees. Zionism has borrowed its concepts and tools of domination from European colonial architecture and these are being put into practice to discipline and punish both the Palestinians and the Oriental Jews (Mizrahis) who migrated to Israel from Iraq, Yemen and other Asian and African countries. The discrimination, racism, denial of opportunity and equality to Palestinians both inside and outside Israel and similar treatment to Mizrahis leads one to question Zionism as an ideology based on a certain ethnocratic systems of exclusion practiced in spatial frames and grids. This is put into context by Edward Said in his essay *Zionism from the Standpoint of its Victims.* Ella Shohat who herself has been a victim of Zionism's exclusionary practices, in her essay titled *Sephardim in Israel: Zionism from the Standpoint of its Jewish Victims* diagnoses the Zionist imagination from the standpoint of Mizrahi Jews who have been discriminated against since the creation of the state of Israel. Both Edward Said and Ella Shohat develop a critique of Zionism's single trajectory of power, its history, its culture, and its politics from the standpoint of Palestinians and Arab Jews.

Edward Said's intellectual development and critique of Zionism's power developed as a result of his personal experience of dislocations, placelessness and exile. The experience of being *Out Of Place* as the title of his memoir suggests, his life lived in both parts of the globe led Said to develop a critique of power from the point of view of a public intellectual who is always at the 'margins' of power. Said's experience led him to adopt Gramsci's definition of an intellectual as someone organically linked to society as against Julien Benda's definition of the intellectual as 'philosopher king'. In his book, *The Representations of the Intellectual,* Said subscribes to the views of Turgenev's hero, Bazarov in *Fathers and Sons* who is a nihilist to the core, hating all the systems, not subscribing to the values of the family or institutions. In Said's view an intellectual creates a 'destabilizing effect; he sets off seismic shocks, he jolts people' (Said 1996: 56). Another prototype of an intellectual in Saidian context would be that of Theodore Adorno who spent an exilic life in the United States as a result of Nazi rule in Germany. For Adorno, as he expresses in his memoir, *Minima Moralia: Reflections on a Damaged Life,* house or dwelling is a 'past' thing in the age modernist devastation. Reflecting on his own life as displaced and dispossessed, aligning himself with Turgenev's Bazarov and Adorno's critical writings, Said develops the idea of the exilic intellectual derived from the idea of displacement. 'For the intellectual exilic displacement means being liberated from the usual career' and 'exile means that you are always going to be marginal' (ibid.: 62). Ella Shohat argues that Edward Said's critique 'conjures up the Diasporic Palestinian narrative as itself historically intertwined with post-Enlightenment European-Jewish identity and sketches the ambivalent position of the Palestinian intellectual in the West as again both insider and outsider' (Shohat 2006: 287).

The success of Zionism in creating the state of Israel is very much appreciated and lauded by the liberals in the West but in Said's point of view, 'very little is said about what Zionism entailed for non-Jews' — millions of Palestinians 'who happened to have encountered it' (Said 1992: 57). The fact that Palestinians were made to 'pay and suffer' for an idea like Zionism which was not their creation but that of someone else's outside their geography and imagination, entails, according to Said, the absence of 'the very things that are centrally important' (ibid.: 57). Zionism, Said argues, should be studied structurally in two ways — 'genealogically,' 'as a practical system of accumulation', and 'displacement'. The western liberal discourse of equating anti-Zionism as 'anti-Semitic,' Said argues, is the heart of the problem.

Zionism was born out of the elemental vision of the 19th century imperialism whose master craftsmen saw the whole globe as an 'empty territory'. Imperialism, as Said argues, 'is a political philosophy whose aim and purpose of being is the territorial expansion and its legitimization' and 'laying claim to an idea and laying claim to a territory' are the 'different sides' of a single 'constitutive activity' buttressed and legitimized by the 'authority of science' (ibid.: 73). The political philosophy of Zionism and imperialism as Said further argues, 'are epistemologically, hence historically and politically coterminous in their views of resident natives' (ibid.: 83). There is a thread connecting the writings of George Eliot, Joseph Conrad to name a few and the

Zionist imagination in the works of Moses Hess, Theodore Herzl, Chaim Weizmann, Yehoshua Porath and others. Said beautifully dissects the geographical imagination of 'empty' land or territory in the writings of both the western liberals and the Zionists. Land and its people were intimately connected with racist and civilizational tones where 'a civilized man, it was believed, could cultivate the land because it meant something to him' and 'for an uncivilized people, land was either farmed badly or it was left to rot' (ibid.: 75). It is this idea of space, as Said states, that provided a justification for colonial expansion coupled with a civilizing mission of 'redeeming the land, resettling the natives, civilizing them, taming their savage customs, turning them into useful beings' (ibid.: 76).

Zionism's connection with the British culture can be seen working in George Eliot's *Daniel Deronda* (1876). Eliot makes a case for Zion's fulfilment of a national home in the following passage through the voice of Mordecai Ezra Cohen, the spiritual guru of Daniel Deronda:

> The soul of Judaism is not dead. Revive the organic centre: let the unity of Israel which has made the growth and form of its religion be an outward reality. Looking towards a land and polity, our dispersed people in all the ends of the earth may share the dignity of a national life which has a voice among the people of the East and the West- which will plant the wisdom and skill of our race so that it may be, as of old, a medium of transmission and understanding. Let that come to pass, and the living warmth will vanish, not in the lawlessness of the renegade, but in the illumination of great facts which widen feeling, and make all knowledge alive as the young offspring of beloved memories (ibid.: 63).

As the Jews have plenty of wealth to 'redeem' the land from the natives and 'skill of the statesman' and 'tongue of the orator' to convince them, Eliot goes on

> Then our race shall have an organic centre, a heart and brain to watch and guide and execute; *the outraged Jew shall have a defense in the court of the nations*, as the outraged Englishman of America. And the world will gain as Israel gains. For there will be a community in the van of the East which carries the culture and the sympathies of every great nation in its bosom; *there will be a land set for a halting-place of enmities, a neutral ground for the East as Belgium is for the West* [Emphasis in the original] (ibid.: 64)

While the case for Zionism is made in Eliot's novel, Said argues that there is an inherent silence and 'total absence of any thought about the actual inhabitants of the East, Palestine in particular' (ibid.: 65). For Eliot, Zionism 'will be a bridge between those warring representatives of the East and the West' (ibid.: 64). Eliot's imagination of a Zionist state as a bridge between the East and the West is echoed by Herzl in his Essay, *The Jewish State* (1896). Herzl's ideas here seem to be repeated by Eliot:

> Palestine is our ever-memorable historic home. The very name of Palestine would attract our people with a force of marvelous potency. If His Majesty the Sultan were to give us Palestine, we could in return undertake to regulate the whole finances of Turkey. *We should there form a portion of a rampart of Europe against Asia, an outpost of civilization as opposed to barbarism. We should as a neutral State remain in contact with all Europe, which would have to guarantee our existence.* The sanctuaries of Christendom would be safeguarded by assigning to them an extra-territorial status such as is well-known to the law of nations. We should form a guard of honor about these sanctuaries, answering for the fulfillment of this duty with our existence. This guard of honor would be the great symbol of the solution of the Jewish question after eighteen centuries of Jewish suffering [Emphasis added] (Herzl 1989: 13).

And here is Chaim Weizmann writing about a land where Palestinians do not exist. For Weizmann the right to cultivate the land and make it 'bloom' is reserved for the Zionists as if the land of Palestine was waiting for the redeemer. In his autobiography, *Trial and Error: The Autobiography of Chaim Weizmann,* he writes,

> It seems as if God has covered the soil of Palestine with rocks and marshes and sand, so that its beauty can only be brought out by those who love it and will devote their lives to healing its wounds (Said 1992: 85).

The master craftsman and storyteller of European colonialism, Joseph Conrad sees the whole world as an 'empty' space where his hero of *The Heart of Darkness,* Marlow is full of

> passion for maps. I would look for hours at South America, Africa or Australia, and lose myself in all the glories of exploration. At that time there were many blank spaces on the earth, and I saw one that looked particularly inviting on a map (but they all look like that) I would put my finger on it and say, when I grow up I will go there (ibid.: 77).

Said draws a lineage of geographical imaginations from British to Zionist thought over Palestine. 'Zionism,' writes Said, 'essentially saw Palestine as the European imperialist did, as an empty territory paradoxically "filled" with ignoble or perhaps even dispensable natives' (ibid.: 81). Carrying forward the colonial imagination, Flinders Petrie saw Arabs as 'disgustingly incapable as most other savages' (Said 1992: 80) comparing Arabs to native Red Indians and Maoris. The essential feature of colonialism is the 'thingification' of the natives, their land and their culture which transforms the colonized subjects into an 'instrument of production' (Césaire 2010: 42). The zoological fantasy of designating animality to the native populations, turning them into 'savages' and referring to them in zoological terms is the hallmark of colonization as Fanon and Césaire would argue. Apart from referring to Palestinians in bestiary terms, a metaphor of disease was also invented by Zionism. 'The metaphor of the Palestinian', Ilan Pappé writes, 'as a disease that had to be cured continued to feature in the official discourses in 1970s' (Pappé 2014: 33). Zionism also adopted the 'typology' of the European colonial attitudes of 'fearsome Orient confronting the Occident' as Said argues, but what made Zionism more complex and distinct was that as a product of the European colonialism itself, Zionism 'confronted the Orient *in* the Orient' (Said 1992: 89). What seems strange and paradoxical in Said's view is the question of victimization. The Jews who were once victims themselves of the European anti-Semitism and holocaust by the Nazi regime turned up to be oppressors of 'Palestinian Arabs and Oriental Jews' (ibid.: 69). The fact that the Palestinians have not reconciled or come to terms with Zionism is because of its 'uncompromisingly exclusionary, discriminatory, colonialist praxis' (ibid.: 69). Said recognized the suffering of the Jewish people. He advocated on the basis of sufferings of the two communities, a bi-national state. He said, 'we cannot coexist as two communities of detached and uncommunicatingly separate suffering. There is suffering and injustice enough for everyone' (Rose 2007: 195).

Who is to be remembered and who is to be forgotten? Who will be remembered in history? How should history be written? What happens when memory and history are conceived in singularity and homogeneity? Is there a single story or are there *stories* or is there a history or are there *histories*? How does geography influence history and memory? As a product of the European colonial project, Zionism as an ideology was able to establish a 'national home' for the 'Jewish people' by forging a singular identity-—that of European Jews, while negating other Jewish identities. Zionism in its foundation carried the same missionary zeal of disciplining and civilizing the native populations as other European colonial projects did in Asia, Africa and Latin America.

Zionism in its construction of nation based on ethnicity has not only displaced and marginalized the Palestinians but a section of its own Jewish population who are until today being discriminated against. The inhuman treatment, denial, racism, subjugation, harassment and other forms of injustice meted out to Mizrahis or the Oriental Jews, 'Israel's internal others' (Massad 2006) throughout its history has opened another can of worms. Within its expanding boundaries Israel has created a 'semi-colonized nation-within-a-nation' (Shohat 1988: 2) in which a majority of the population of Sephardim is ruled by a tiny minority of European Jews. From George Eliot to Zionist leaders a discourse has been created about Palestine as 'a land without people' ready to be populated, nurtured and brought into existence as a part of the first world 'for a people without land'. Zionism as a discourse in the same manner as Ella Shohat through her studies on the subject has shown, carried the same Orientalist tone while defining the Oriental Jews. The acceptance of the Oriental Jews in Israeli society was a matter of concern since this part of the Jewish diaspora had its genesis and origin in a geography which was not white or European in character. They migrated or were forced to migrate to Israel from the 'accursed' geographies of Asian and African countries.

Taking cue from Frantz Fanon's idea of the relation between the colonizer and the colonized in *The Wretched of the Earth* and Aimé Césaire's *Discourse on Colonialism,* Shohat delves into Zionist historiography and culture to expose the bias and racism of Ashkenazi dominated Israeli politics. Ella Shohat clinically exposes the East/West dichotomy in Zionist discourse where a majority of the population is of Eastern origin and yet Israel defines itself historically as a part of the West. Israel as a country geographically located in the East as part of the West Asian region does not consider itself as a part of the third world. This paradox as Shohat mentions, 'is that it presumed to "end a diaspora" characterized by ritualistic nostalgia for the East, only to found a state ideologically and geopolitically oriented exclusively toward the West' (Shohat 1999: 7). By presenting itself as 'redeemer' of Arab Jews from Arab 'captors' the mainstream Zionists set out to teach modern European values to Arab Jews 'handicapped as they have been by their Oriental, illiterate, despotic, sexist, and generally pre-modern formations in their land of origin, as well as by their propensity for generating large families' (Shohat 1988: 3). Arab Jews in Israel have been subjected to the same Oriental discourse and power relations of the master/slave oppositionality 'expressed by politicians, social scientists, educators, writers, and the mass media' (ibid.: 3).

On April 22, 1949, journalist Arye Gelblum while reporting for *Haaretz* on the mass immigration of Jews from Arab countries, wrote,

> This is immigration of a race we have not yet known in the country...We are dealing with people whose primitivism is at a peak, whose level of knowledge is one of virtually absolute ignorance, and worse, who have little talent for understanding anything intellectual. Generally, they are only slightly better than the general level of the Arabs, Negroes, and Berbers in the same regions. In any case, they are at an even lower level than what we knew with regard to the former Arabs of the Eretz Israel... These Jews also lack roots in Judaism, as they are totally subordinated to the play of savage and primitive instincts... As with the Africans you will find card games for money, drunkenness and prostitution. Most of them have serious eye, skin and sexual diseases, without mentioning robberies and thefts (Shohat 1988: 4).

Gelblum as Shohat writes, concludes the report on the basis of the advice of a French diplomat and sociologist, echoing the colonial vision working in Ashkenazi attitude towards the Arab Jews. Gelblum goes on to advise Israel against making a 'fatal mistake' the French made in their own country; he warns against opening their gates 'too wide to Africans', as a 'certain kind of human material' will erase Israel's image and turn it into a 'Levantine state' thereby sealing the 'fate' of Israel (Shohat 1988: 4). Portrayal of the other in zoological terms was a part of the Orientalist mindset which the Zionist imagination borrowed from its European counterpart. 'The colonizer', as Shohat notes, is 'unable to speak of the colonized without resorting to bestiary' (ibid.: 6). Shohat observes that this statement is not an isolated incident as successive Israeli leaders have shown contempt for Arab Jews. David Ben-Gurion stated, 'we do not want Israelis to become Arabs. We are in duty bound to fight against the spirit of the Levant, which corrupts individuals and societies, and preserve the authentic Jewish values as they crystallized in the Diaspora' (ibid.: 4). Joining the line of racist imagination is Arthur Ruppin, a labour Zionist who according to Shlomo Sand was a 'confirmed Darwinist' and was sceptical about the mass immigration of Oriental Jews. For Ruppin, the Yemenite workers have 'the touch of Arab blood, and they have a very dark colour' (Sand 2010: 14). In his book titled, *The Jews of Today,* Ruppin stated, 'the spiritual and intellectual status of these Jews [referring to immigration of Jews from Yemen, Morocco and the Caucasus] is so low that an immigration *en masse* would lower the general cultural standard of the Jews in Palestine and would be bad from several points of view' (ibid.: 263). Ruppin was also against intermarriage even among the Oriental and Occidental Jews because 'the race character is lost' and the offspring of these mixed marriages would not produce 'remarkable gifts' (ibid.: 263). Sand notes, 'the profoundly Eurocentric outlook was even stronger than the concepts of the Jewish race, and this simplistic Orientalism was common in all the Zionist movements' (ibid.: 263). The biological distinction, observes Sand, 'sought to serve the project of ethnic nationalist consolidation in taking over of an imaginary ancient homeland' (ibid.: 265).

The 'class positioning' was central in defining and distinguishing an Arab worker from a European Ashkenazi worker as Shohat observes. From the beginning, Oriental Jews were perceived by mainstream

Zionists as the cheap source of labour replacing the Palestinian labour. Shohat observes that Yemenite workers were presented just as 'workers', 'primeval matter' while Ashkenazi workers were considered to be 'creative' and 'idealists' with a vision to make something new. The 'economic-political interest,' observes Shohat, motivated the 'selective ingathering' as 'young and healthy people' were selected for immigration to Israel (Shohat 1988: 14). 'Deluded' by the Zionist slogan of 'land of milk and honey,' ten thousand Sephardim were allowed as a policy of 'engineered immigration' to enter Palestine before World War II (ibid.: 15). Shohat observes the condition of the Sephardim labourers, thus,

> they were put to work mainly as agricultural day-laborers in extremely harsh conditions to which, despite Zionist mythology, they were *decidedly not* accustomed. *Yemenite families were crowded together in stables, pastures, windowless cellers (for which they had to pay) or simply obliged to live in the fields.* Unsanitary conditions and malnutrition caused widespread disease and death, especially of infants. The Zionist Association employers and the Ashkenazi landowners and their overseers treated the Yemenite Jews brutally, at times abusing even the women and children... Labor Zionism, through the Histadrut, managed to prevent Yemenites from owning land or joining cooperatives, thus limiting them to the role of wage-earners. As with the Arab workers, the dominant "socialist" ideology within Zionism thus provided no guarantee against ethno-centrism. While presenting Palestine as an empty land to be transformed by Jewish labor, the Founding Fathers presented Sephardim as passive vessels to be shaped by the revivifying spirit of Promethean Zionism... *the visionary dream of a Zionist Jewish State were not designed for the Sephardim* [Emphasis added] (ibid.: 15).

A zone of dependency was created by dividing Israel— a prosperous North with European domination and a ghettoized South reserved for Oriental Jews to provide labour power and other manual works. The wealth generated as a result of economic exploitation went into the hands of prosperous Northern Europeans who wielded power over major institutions of the country. Israeli authorities created '*Ayarot Pituha*' (Development Towns) mainly in rural areas and frontier regions to thwart the Arab attacks. Thus ethnic segregation was practiced from the beginning: Northern Zone for Ashkenazim and underdeveloped Southern Zone for Sephardim reminiscent of the working class conditions of the twentieth century Italy in the works of Antonio Gramsci's *Prison Notebooks*.

Along with the exploitation of cheap labour, exclusion and racial segregation practiced by Israeli authorities, the Oriental Jews became victims to the messianic process of modernizing. On June 30, 1986 a group of Mizrahi Jews under the Banner of 'The Public Committee for the Discovery of the Missing Yemenite Children' held a massive protest demonstration. The Israeli media did not report the demonstration. About six hundred Yemenite babies were transferred to Ashkenazi couples so that these children would be brought up in a European fashion. A ring of Israeli doctors, nurses and social workers were behind this ploy. The whereabouts of these missing children were mired in controversy as the doctors reported to children's parents that they had died and the experts came out with a statement that the deaths of these children were 'common and natural.' The doctors issued fake death certificates and handed them to their parents. Despite voices being raised for decades, the Israeli authorities remained silent on the issue (ibid.: 17). The act of separating babies from their natural mothers 'from a space of premodernity to that of modernity' to be raised by Western standards and norms was considered 'logical, rational and scientific' and a 'redemptive' act. 'In this intersection of race, gender, and class, the displaced Jews from Muslim countries became victims of the logic of progress, bearing the marks of its pathologies on their bodies' (Shohat 2003: 65-66).

In her essay titled *Rupture and Return: Zionist Discourse and the Study of Arab Jews* (2003), Ella Shohat proposes a *multichronotopic* perspective of time and space focusing on 'dynamic palimpsest of identity formations' through the grids of *dislocations, displacements, dischronicity, dissonance and disciplining.* She argues that along with the Zionist construction and the invention of the Jewish people based on a linear historiography, Mizrahi identity too was 'invented' by Zionism (Shohat 2003: 50).[2] Shohat observes that the invention of Zionism and its 'project of ingathering of exiles' created 'dislocations' resulting in a 'series of traumatic ruptures and exilic identity formations' (ibid.: 52). The Jewishness within the Arab culture 'was a part of larger Judeo-Islamic cultural fabric' (ibid.: 52) that came into conflict with the homogenous and dominant conception defined by Israel in which anything concerning or related to Islam and Arab culture was thought to be a derogatory practice. The Zionization and the creation of a single homogenous community of Jews by a dominant ideology had put the whole Arab Jewish community in conflict with Arab nationalism. Caught between two nationalist positions, Shohat argues that the 'set of affiliations gradually changed, resulting in a transformed cultural

2. On the invention of the Mizrahi identity, Shohat observes, 'By provoking the geographical dispersal of the Jews from the Muslim world, by placing them in a new situation on the ground, by attempting to reshape their identity as simply "Israeli," by disdaining and trying to uproot their Easterness, by discriminating against them as a group, Zionism obliged Arab Jews to redefine themselves in relation to new ideological polarities, thus provoking the aporias of an identity constituted out of its own ruins. Jews in the Muslim world always thought of themselves as "Jews," but their Jewishness was assumed as part of the Judeo-Islamic cultural fabric. With Zionism, that set of affiliations changed, resulting in a transformed semantics of belonging. But the delegitimization of Middle Eastern culture has boomeranged in the face of Euro-Israel: out of the massive encounter that has taken place between Jews from such widely separated regions as the Maghreb and Yemen emerged a new overarching umbrella identity, what came to be called "the Mizrahim"' (Shohat 1999: 13).

semantics' had put the Mizrahim into 'terminological crisis' (ibid.: 52)[3].

Geographically, the Jewish community in Iraq has been a part of Iraqi culture for ages. The collusion between Zionist underground forces working in Iraq and the Iraqi government, the propaganda created by Istiklal party had put the Jewish community in Iraq in a fix. Majority of the Jewish people were anti-Zionists and were not willing to migrate. Under utter panic and confusion the Jews were forced to migrate and leave Iraq. The official Zionist historiography termed this forced expulsion as a part of naturalized *aliya*. 'The official term *aliya*,' as Shohat observes, 'is multiply misleading. It suggests a commitment to Zionism, when in fact the majority of Jews—and certainly Jews within the Levant —were decidedly not Zionists. Zionist discourse normalized the telos of a Jewish nation-state; the move toward its borders was represented as the ultimate Jewish act' (ibid.: 55-56). The Arab leaders and intellectuals failed in assuring the Jewish community's security and also sidelined the distinction between a Jew and a Zionist (ibid.: 55-56). The term *aliya* (ascendancy) is an ideologically loaded term affiliated with the project of Zionism. Shohat sees the immigration of Iraqi Jews as a case of 'dislocation' rather than a 'choice' or 'desire' since immigration was not preferred at a larger scale. It was more a case of *yerida* (social descent) rather than *aliya* (ascent) (ibid.: 57-58).

3. There are innumerable terms used in debates and discourses concerning the Oriental Jews. Shohat lists them in detail; Sephardim; non-Ashkenazi Jews; Jews of Islam; Arab Jews; Middle Eastern, West Asian, or North African Jews; Asian and African Jews; non European Jews; Third World Jews; Levantine Jews; Jews of the Mediterranean; *Maghrebian* and *Mashreqian* Jews (from the western and eastern parts of the Arab world); *Bnei Edot Ha Mizrah* (descendants of the Eastern communities); *yotzei artzot arav ve-ha-Islam* (those who left Arab and Muslim countries); Blacks; Israel ha-Shniya (Second Israel); Mizrahiyim, or Mizrahim; or Iraqi Jews, Iranian Jews, Kurdish Jews, Palestinian Jews, Moroccan Jews, and so forth (Shohat 2003: 52-53). Among the host of terminologies, Shohat uses the term 'Arab Jew' thereby retaining geography as a part of identity so as to distinguish it from a general historical connotation of a *Jewish history* paving a way for *histories* rather than history. In an ideological agreement of multiple histories and geographies with Shohat I will be using the term *Arab Jew* throughout the book.

> The permission to leave—as in the case of Iraqi Jews—did not allow for a possible return either of individuals or of the community. Therefore, even the term *immigration* does not account for that massive crossing of borders. Iraqi Jews, for example, had to give up their citizenship (*al-tasqit*), losing their right to return. Within Israel, for at least four decades, performing even a symbolic return within the public sphere—the expression of nostalgia for an Arab past —became taboo. The propagandistic description of the dislocation of Arab Jews as "population exchange," which supposedly justifies the creation of Palestinian refugees, meanwhile, is also fundamentally problematic... *While for the Jews from the Muslim world the Land of Israel/Palestine was continuous with their cultural geography, the Eurocentric construct of the State of Israel on that land required discontinuity*. The passage into the political space of Israel initiated Jews from Arab and Muslim lands into a new process within which *they were transformed, almost overnight, into a new racialized ethnic identity*. Therefore, a critical scholarship cannot afford to assume the Zionist master narrative of choice and desire; rather it needs to look into the deep anxious ambivalences generated by partition and the scars it left on the psyche of the displaced [Emphasis added] (ibid.: 58).

The politics of the 'population exchange' suggests that the Arab Jews were unwanted guests in Israel which justified the exclusion of the Palestinians. Moreover, the concern and the drive for 'exchanging' Arab Jews for the Palestinians were based on political-economic advantages. If the Zionist historiography accepts the Arab Jews as a natural part of *aliya* then why were they forced by Zionists to immigrate to Israel in the first place? The 'population exchange' was a 'thing-thing' relation where the political economy of the state was the driving force. The sheer fact of the use of force denotes a politics of population where the major concerns of the Zionist politics were based on Palestinian depopulation.

Shohat further accepts the truism that all nations are invented but 'some nations, such as Jewish/Israel, are *more* invented than others' (ibid.: 59). The Zionist politics of inventing a common national memory of the cultural past embedded in spatiality was successful in excluding a diverse range of memories especially those of the Arab Jews. By imposing the selective memories of the European past on other identities based on geography, language and associations, Shohat observes that the Zionist historiography and its construction of memory has been involved in a 'state of perennial adrenal anxiety.' Zionist conception of 'Jewish History' presumes a unitary and universal notion of history, rather than a multiplicity of experiences, differing from period to period and from context to context (ibid.: 59-60). What was expelled from memory was a common past of Judeo-Islamic culture and tradition which flourished in Spain. The year 1492 marks another expulsion in world history. Although the year 1492 is celebrated across the Euro-American geographies as the mark of a beginning of a new world, there is not a single word of condemnation of atrocities committed by Columbus on the Moors of Iberia. 'Your Highnesses completed the war against the Moors,' wrote Columbus addressed to the Spanish Empress, 'after having chased all the Jews... and sent me to the said regions of India in order to convert the people there to our holy faith' (Shohat 2014: 90). The Judeo-Islamic multicultural Moorish Spain was erased by 'an early exercise in European "self-purification", sought to expel, or forcibly convert, Muslims and Jews' (ibid.: 91). The Israeli historiography, cultural institutions, media and the [illegible] memory. The selective appropriation and memorialisation of victimization in Europe becomes a teleological force in uniting the diverse Jewish experiences and memories of the past. The following passage by Shohat is worth quoting:

> In this rewriting of history, present-day Muslim-Arabs are merely one more 'non-Jewish' obstacle to the Jewish-Israeli national trajectory. The idea of the unique, common victimization of all Jews at all times provides a crucial underpinning of the official Israeli discourse. The notion of uniqueness precludes analogies and metonymies, thus producing a selective reading of 'Jewish history', one that hijacks the Jews of Islam from their Judeo-Islamic geography, and subordinates it to that of the European-Ashkenazi *shtetl.* This double process entails the performance of commonalities among Jews in the public sphere so as to suggest a homogenous national past, while silencing any more globalized and historicized narrative that would see Jews not simply through their religious commonalities but also in relation to their contextual cultures, institutions, and practices (ibid.: 94-95).

Edward Said's study of Zionism from the viewpoint of power/knowledge in his pioneering work on Orientalism as a discourse made intrusions into Israel, especially in the Mizrahi academic circles. Saidian influence can be easily seen in Shohat's works. Zionism was seen by Mizrahi scholars as carrying the same Oriental and racist imaginations towards the Mizrahis. Apart from Shohat, Sami Shalom Chetrit as a part of the Moroccan Jewish community in his scholarly works and through his activism challenged the Zionist imagination and racist attitude towards Arab Jews. The Mizrahi Jewish scholars and intellectuals like Shohat, Chetrit and others identify themselves with the Palestinian cause because of their spatio-cultural affiliation and rootedness in Arab culture. As Ilan Pappé suggests, these scholars 'were seeking their roots as Arabs, not necessarily as Jews' (Pappé 2014: 192). In his poem, *I am an Arab Refugee, 2004,* Chetrit wrote,

> When I hear Fayruz singing, 'I shall never forget thee, Palestine',

> I swear to you with my right hand
> that at once I am a Palestinian.
> All of a sudden I know:
> I am an Arab refugee
> and, if not,
> let my tongue cleave to the roof of my mouth. (Pappé 2014: 193)

Chetrit's community's 'angst and frustration', as Pappé notes, 'come through best in his poems' (ibid.: 193).

Reading the Unconscious Spaces of Zionism: The 'Crackpot' and Psychoanalysis

In her essay, *The Jewish State: Fifty Years After, Where Have Herzl's Politics Led?* Hannah Arendt diagnoses the inherent dilemma of Herzl's vision of creating a Zionist state in Palestine. The 'extreme self esteem', writes Arendt, 'mixed with self doubt is not a rare phenomenon; it is usually the sign of the "crackpot"' (Arendt 2007: 375). This inherent dilemma of the founding of the Zionist state carries within itself a 'risk with utopia that it might not quite believe in itself' (Rose 2005: 63). Herzl was a 'depressive' with constant mood swings as Rose points out from Herzl's diary entry of 1879 where he wrote, 'I have much cause to complain about the changes in my moods, to exalt to high heaven, to be deadly depressed, soon to delude myself with hope . . . then again to die but soon to be rejected by death . . . Pain is the basic feeling of life' (ibid.: 64). *Der Judenstaat* or *The Jewish State* was produced by Herzl in a 'state of mental intoxification' which took him 'beyond the limits of consciousness' (ibid.: 64). Rose continues, 'the depression of Zionism' (ibid.: 65) was not confined to Herzl alone. The future president of Israel also fell in line. In a letter to Leo Motzkin, Weizmann wrote, '[My health] is not good. As a matter of fact I went to see the doctor yesterday. He diagnosed neurasthenia and weakness of the respiratory organs. *Übermüdung und Überreizung* (overfatigue and overexcitement)' (ibid.: 65). A certain kind of sickness was a necessary element in the construction of Zionism. 'Zionism could be forged only in a state "beyond consciousness" (. . . the making of the nation cannot be grasped by a conscious mind)' (ibid.: 65-66). For Herzl and Weizmann and others who followed, Zionism became a 'conjuring act' of the unconscious (ibid.: 67). Rose lays bare the contradictions, madness and the dilemma of the foundation of Israel through her psychoanalytic study of Zionism. In her view, 'psychoanalysis can help us to understand the symptom of statehood', as 'there is something inside the very process upholding the state as a reality which threatens and exceeds it' (Rose 1996: 10). In escaping from modernity's wrath, in the quest of a nation as Rose suggests, Israel while 'displacing the Palestinians produced on the spot a new people without statehood' thereby, 'to engender within its own boundaries the founding conditions from which it fled' (ibid.: 13). Statelessness as Hannah Arendt saw it was not a problem specific for Jews. Arendt saw statelessness as a universal phenomenon of modernity, a 'recurrent 20th-century predicament of the nation-state' (Butler 2007), and nationalisms, as the case of India and Palestine suggests. Arendt's 'skepticism towards Zionism' as Butler notes is grounded in ontology. Arendt in her book, *The Origins of Totalitarianism,* viewed that the 'solution of the Jewish question merely produced a new category of refugees, the Arabs, thereby increasing the number of stateless and rightless by another 700,000 to 800,000 people' (Butler 2007: 26). For Rose, 'Zionism is a violation of reality that knows its own delusions. And runs with it' (Rose 2005: 16). Herzl and Weizmann were literary figures before becoming committed Zionists. Rose charts out delusional and fantastic ideas in their literary creation. She shows a clear distinction between their political pamphleteering and fictional writings. If their political writings showed 'the triumph of the will', their literary productions were symptomatic of far greater danger of a 'messianic redemption' of the land. Herzl's novel, *Altneuland (The Old New Land)* is a departure from his *Der Judenstaat.*

> But Altneuland was a utopian fantasy. There would be no ownership of land, no control of sacred spaces; all humans, regardless of faith or origin, would have equal status in an ideal world. The Arab, Reshid Bey, welcomes the Jews without hesitation as the bearers of a new and prosperous existence for all the inhabitants of Palestine. Sixty years after the creation of Israel, there could not be a wider gap between the cruel reality of Israel today and Herzl's dream (Rose 2008).

Displacement is at the core of Zionism. Israel might have laid foundation to a state exclusively for the Jewish diaspora with exclusive 'right of return' but as a state it could not diminish displacement as a 'psychic' category from its foundational structure. 'The baggage of mind' moves with people wherever they go and 'you carry your enemies within you,' and 'nothing as psychoanalysis will testify, is ever left behind' (Rose 2007: 41). Even as people might be moving alone, somewhere in the dark corners of the mind, 'we see people on the move at least partly as sleepwalkers, trundling through each other's dark night' (ibid.: 45). The foundation of the state of Israel is full of such displacements as Rose suggests. The identification can be seen in Smilansky Yizhar's novella, *Hirbet Hiza* (1948). A young Israeli soldier witnesses the Palestinian Nakba and he is at once 'struck with displacement', to use Mourid Barghouti's phrase. He sees 'the exile (*Galut*) of his own people unfolding before his eyes' where 'something suddenly became clear to me in a flash. At once I saw everything in a new, clear light- Galut. This is Galut. Galut is like this. This is what Galut looks like' (ibid.: 48). Ram Levy, an Israeli filmmaker translated Yizhar's *Hirbet Hiza* into a film. In a conversation with Levy, Yizhar revealed that the novella was based on the reality of a Palestinian village which was destroyed and its people expelled. Levy in search of the village found one in the West Bank which exactly looked like the village depicted by Yizhar in *Hirbet Hiza* (Pappé 2014: 220- 222).

Even after the establishment of the state of the Israel in 1948, there was something within its walls that disturbed its people who migrated from different parts of Europe. Something was wrong with the foundation. In his autobiography Amos Oz writes similarly about the condition of his mother. Fania Mussman, Oz's mother was somehow not comfortable and there was something unsettling about Israel which disturbed her leading her to commit suicide. The trauma subsisted even after the establishment of the state of Israel. Oz's mother 'found no interest in Jerusalem' and the 'Zionist fervor passed my mother by' (Oz 2004: 262-263). Suicides became a commonplace as the foundations of the Jewish State was being laid. Rose quotes Shulamith Hareven who in her 1988 essay, *Israel: The First Forty Years* wrote, 'the early years of Zionist settlement in Palestine are replete with stories of suicide, collapse, bodily and mental anguish; the sound of weeping at night is an almost permanent counterpoint to the refrain of pioneering Zionism' (Rose 2007: 51). The contradiction of Israel, its inner turmoil can be felt in *My Michael,* the novel written by Amos Oz in 1968. Hannah Gonen, the heroine of the novel can be seen withdrawing into a state of melancholy in an 'alien city', Jerusalem. Hannah as a mentor guides two Arab boys in her colonial adventures and is paradoxically haunted by them with 'machine guns on their shoulders' in her dream (Oz 2011: 78). Hannah drifts into a state of loneliness, withdraws from her husband into a world of fantasies and repressed desires. Does Hannah represent internal contradictions of Israel? Jacqueline Rose comments, 'seeing the enemy as outside threat only, Israel was sowing the seeds of long-term damage within' (Rose 2005: 72). 'Oz therefore allows the young girl to act out the reality of colonial power between Jew and Arab even during the mandate period before Israel was born' (Rose 2008). In Rose's view, Oz painted a picture of what was to come later, a state bent on its own destruction through violence.

David Grossman, a contemporary of Oz is another literary figure who paints the picture of Israel as a 'failed state' (Rose 2007: 112). Grossman is a courageous novelist who tried to break the boundaries and see what a Palestinian feels about the state of Israel. In his collection of essays, *Death as a Way of Life,* Grossman writes, 'an entire nation is in a coma. Six million people have allowed their mind, their will, their judgment to degenerate into infuriating criminal passivity' and 'when we emerge from the cocoon that encloses us, it is liable to be too late' (ibid.: 112). In his speech at Rabin Memorial in 2006, Grossman questions Israel's policies once more. He asks, 'How could it be that a people with such powers of creativity, renewal and vivacity as ours, a people that knew how to rise from the ashes time and again, finds itself today, despite its great military might, at such a state of laxity and inanity, a state 'where it is the victim once more, but this time its own victim, of its anxieties, its short-sightedness' (Grossman 2006). The state of Israel 'born out of monumental visions' in Oz's view is seen by Grossman as a victim of its own 'anxieties' and 'short sightedness'. Grossman appeals to his people to see Palestinians 'not through the sights of a gun, and not behind a closed roadblock', but to see Palestinians as 'a people that are tortured no less than us. An oppressed, occupied people bereft of hope' (ibid.). In another novel *Sleeping on a Wire,* Grossman paints the contradiction of the Jewish state from the point of view of two minorities in Israel: The Palestinians and the Arab Jews. In *The Yellow Wind* (1988), Grossman talks about the Palestinian predicament in refugee camps through his interviews and dialogues. Despite his contending views on Israel, Grossman remains a committed Zionist in his views. He does not want to remain as a part of the 'Jewish minority in Israel' as it will erase the whole idea of the Jewish state. He wants a 'partial justice' for both

Israelis and Palestinians. Rose translates this statement as: 'Justice is partial' (Rose 2007: 119). Grossman does not want complete justice as International Law and other conventions allow— the right of return of the Palestinians and a state of their own. Such justice in the case of the Palestinians will destroy the dream of a state exclusively for the Jewish people. In Rose's view Grossman is like a child 'badly let-down'. The Zionist ideology views that the geography is absolute and solid like a container where you can fit anything without any idea that the container vomits. Spaces are not absolute; they are rather abstract and fluid, always in motion. Grossman as a novelist understands these complexities but still clings to the idea of a state based on exclusion. 'Our space', as Lefebvre (1991: 97) comments, 'has strange effects. For one thing it unleashes desire', then it also seeks revenge for that desire in terms of shocks and ruptures. Spaces also produce after-effects of that desire in terms death. Leo Tolstoy can be our guide here. Tolstoy's hero, Pahom, a peasant in his story, *How Much Land does a Man Need?* in the quest of desiring more and more land for himself, dies vomiting blood. Desire and death are then the two extreme effects of space. Ari Shavit, a commentator in the Israeli daily *Haaretz* sees the end of the Israeli state in its spatial practices. He shares the same concern as David Grossman. 'We see the delegitimization, the demography, the spoilage. We see that more is less. We see that having it all isn't what it was cut out to be; that if we don't draw a border for the Jewish state, there will be no Jewish state' (Shavit 2014). These are the contradictions that the Israel as a state does not understand but its people do. There is not only a single Israel, but there are many Israels within Israel and the commentator is worried about the fate of Israel building settlements here and there, occupying a space here and occupying a space there. The fear of a nation in danger or catastrophe looms large in Israeli psyche. Shavit writes, 'sane Israel is indifferent, loony Israel gets to lead us to the brink of catastrophe. Not because of an act of God but because we are weak-willed and dispirited we allow the wacky fringe groups to take over the national agenda. We let lunatics take us to dark places' (ibid.).

The psychological trauma of Israel as 'failed state' has been captured beautifully by Jacqueline Rose (2004). Is Israel caught up by Pahomian Syndrome of desire whose ultimate end is death as the story of Tolstoy suggests? Rose (2004) quotes David Grossman from his novel, *Death as a Way of Life* as saying, 'When we emerge from the cocoon that encloses us, it is liable to be too late'. What is it, the threat? Is it a symbolic or real? The threat is real. Rose comments, 'Israel has always seen itself as engaged in a struggle for survival – that is its raison d'être. Against the dominant rhetoric, Grossman presents us with a nation that appears – from its violent, stubborn, self-defeating behaviour – to be hell-bent on destroying itself' (ibid.). The trauma Rose depicts and warns against is a consequence of space constructed on the basis of a 'spatial blindness' to use Oren Yiftachel's words. Israelis see the presence of Palestinians all around; inside, outside, periphery, as Rose (1996) would say, but they do not recognize their presence. In one sense the Palestinians are displaced, homeless but in other sense they are housed in the Israeli psyche.

The contradictions which are emerging out of the contestation of identities in a fixed geographical landscape are a result of a politics of spatial imagination which denies space to the other. There was an opposition from a small minority within and outside the Zionist circles who exactly knew that the Zionist idea of a homogenous space was detrimental not only to the Palestinians and the Arabs but to Jews themselves. They understood the complexities of geography. Martin Buber, Judah Magnes, Hans Kohn, Hannah Arendt and Ahad Ha'am warned the Zionists about the consequences of their own politics. Within its boundaries Zionism 'silences dissent that it has most to fear' (Rose 2005: 69). Arendt in *The Jewish State: Fifty Years After, Where have Herzl's Politics Led?* published in *Commentary* in 1945-

46, questions the very foundational aspects of Zionist politics. Arendt comments:

> Today reality has become a nightmare. Looked at through the eyes of Herzl, who from the outside sought a place inside reality into which the Jews could fit and where at the same time they could isolate themselves from it — looked at in this way, reality is horrible beyond the scope of the human imagination and hopeless beyond the strength of human despair ... Some of the Zionist leaders pretend to believe that the Jews can maintain themselves in Palestine against the whole world and that they themselves can preserve in claiming everything or nothing against everybody and everything. However, behind this spurious optimism lurks a despair of everything and a genuine readiness for suicide that can become extremely dangerous should they grow to be the mood and atmosphere of Palestinian politics ... What would happen to Jews all over the world and to Jewish history in the future should we meet with a catastrophe in Palestine (Arendt 2007: 384-387).

Arendt's critique of Herzelian Zionist visions came from a universal perspective of Jewish history. What could have Arendt thought of Ariel Sharon's politics of 'politicide' (the term was coined by Baruch Kimmerling) or Benjamin Netanyahu who keeps on building settlements in the occupied territories despite the warnings from the international community? Arendt, Buber and Magnes argued for a bi-national state from the beginning. In Arendt's view 'any state that failed to have the popular support of all its inhabitants, and that defined citizenship on the basis of religious or national belonging, would be forced to produce a permanent class of refugees' (Butler 2012: 121).

Judah Magnes was another figure who resisted the call for an exclusive Jewish state from the beginning. Since his days as a chancellor of Hebrew University and an important figure in the Zionist movement, Magnes was involved in a series of talks, meetings and deliberations with the Palestinian and Arab leaders for his ideas of a federal structure and bi-national state. Magnes' support for a legislative council which was a major demand by the Arab leaders was criticized by the Zionists but earned him a profound respect among the Arabs (Gonen 1982). Magnes assumed the 'role of a political dissenter and moral gadfly' (ibid.: 3) throughout, to the end of his life. Just few days before the establishment of the state of Israel, Magnes received an invitation from the U.S. State Department through the U.S. Consul in Jerusalem. At the height of his illness, Magnes arrived in the United States to convince the leadership 'to force a cease-fire and prevent both the implementation of the partition plan and the establishment of a Jewish state' (Gonen 1982: 53 & Ilani 2008). Magnes was a lone fighter against the Jewish state. In his diary entry of November 22, 1925, Magnes wrote, '(I) feel greatly alone. Alone in my thoughts about Jews and pacifism and Palestine. No intellectual companionship here' (Gonen 1982). In opposition to Biltmore declaration of 1942, which declared Palestine as a Jewish commonwealth, Magnes commented bitterly, 'the slogan Jewish State or commonwealth is equal, in effect, to a declaration of war by Jews on the Arabs' (ibid.: 46). Like Arendt, the consent of the Arabs in matters pertaining to the Jewish question was paramount for Magnes. In his Address to the Council of the Jewish Agency, Zurich on August 18, 1937, Magnes eloquently said:

> ... everything I have said and done in my life, as far as Palestine is concerned, from the beginning up to this day, has been based upon the fundamental thought that in what we do and what we plan, we should endeavor to get *Arab consent*. And that is the purport of this resolution that we are presenting. This resolution provides for a binational state, if it can be secured with the *consent of Arabs and the Jews* and of the British government [Emphasis added] (ibid.: 329-334).

The partition of Palestine 'would be a misfortune', wrote Magnes in a letter to the editor of the New York Times dated February 17, 1945 titled, 'Compromise for Palestine' (ibid.: 422). Like Ahad Ha'am he did not believe in Israel Zangwill's slogan 'a land without people for a people without land'. He acknowledged the presence of the Palestinians unlike other Zionists who saw Palestinians but preferred not to see. Magnes was a visionary. He saw Israel involved in a labyrinth of violence. Israel was born of violence and continued to perpetrate violence. Magnes personally did not have much to fear but he was afraid for his people, 'afraid for those tender plants' in his country and said, 'I do not want to see the Jewish state conceived and born in warfare' (ibid.). The Zionist idea of nation visualized itself unlike other nations, hermetically sealed from the outside world. Magnes in his pamphlet titled, *'Like All the Nations',* wanted federal style based on the replication of the U.S. Senate and The House of the Representatives. He was of the opinion of a Lower Chamber elected by the whole population, which would give a large Arab majority, and an Upper Chamber, to be elected or appointed upon the basis of the equality of three nationalities, Jewish, Arab, British' (Magnes 1930:8). Magnes did not want an exclusive 'Jewish State' for his people 'that can be maintained in the long run only against the violent opposition of the Arab and Moslem peoples' (ibid.). For Arendt, Judah Magnes was the 'conscience of the Jewish people' and 'being a Jew and being a Zionist, he was simply ashamed of what Jews and Zionists were doing' (Arendt 2007: 451-452).

Influenced by Gandhian politics, Martin Buber was a pacifist and an advocate of 'Cultural Zionism'. In his early years, Buber served as the editor of *Die Welt* (The World), a main organ of the Zionist movement. He was a philosopher of the 'religious existentialism' in the words of Shlomo Sand, 'began his nationalist career as one of the principal molders of the Jewish people as "blood community"', later to become a man of peace and strive to bring about an Arab-Jewish state in Palestine (Sand 2010: 259-260). Along with Hannah Arendt and Judah Magnes he worked for a bi-national state against the political Zionist idea of a Jewish state. Buber was an existentialist. In his major work, *I and Thou*, Buber delves into the relation of *I* [self] with *it* [an object] and *thou* [the other subject]. This dialogue of *I* and its relation to the other becomes a fundamental factor in his Jewish thinking which later culminates in a politics which recognizes the existence of the other. For Buber *I-Thou* relation 'means being chosen and choosing, suffering and action in one; just as any action of the whole being, which means the suspension of all partial actions, and consequently of all sensations of actions grounded only in their particular limitation, is bound to resemble suffering' (Buber 1937: 11). The self is transformed into becoming 'through my relation to the *Thou*' (Buber 1937: 11). *I-Thou* as a whole being cannot take place on 'my own or through the agency of the self', as Buber says, 'nor it can take place without me' (ibid.: 11). In her formulation of *I-You* relation, Judith Butler goes ahead of Buber where she suggests that the *I* in *I-You* relation has to wither away for any emancipatory politics to emerge. 'It is not just a question of finding that what I am depends upon a "you" who is not me, but that my very capacity for attachment and, indeed, for love and receptivity requires a sustained dispossession of this "I"' (Butler 2012: 51). Buber opposed the Zionist idea of the Jewish state as 'the critical and spiritual power of Judaism would be ruined or in Buber's words, "perverted"' (ibid.: 75). Buber's actual position on Jewish State contradicts his philosophy of being as it somehow negates the Palestinians in 'I-Thou' relationships because Zionism as an ideology undermines any coming together of the two. The quest for justification and 'right' of Jews to the land of Palestine led Buber and other Zionists 'to get Gandhi's approval for Zionism', as Gandhi was a leader of the Indian masses and was popular in international circles for his non-violent politics against imperialism and his approval, 'would provide great impetus for the Jewish cause' (Ramakrishnan 2014: 37). Gandhi reproached Jews for not starting a

Satyagraha in Germany against the Nazis and the 'cry for the national home for the Jews' (ibid.: 36) was not appealing to him. In his response to Gandhi, Buber justified Jewish colonization in the garb of 'right to a free land on the other side [Jews] - for those who are hungering for it' (Buber quoted in Ramakrishnan 2014: 39). Marc Ellis (1996) notes that the Buber's correspondence with Gandhi and his later writings on the Israel/Palestine question are 'complex, even colonial'. The Jewish claim to the land, 'stemming from the origins of the Jewish people was connected to his view that Arabs had only a secondary claim to the land' (Ellis 1996: 137). Despite the contradictions in Buber's writings, he was far ahead of the hardcore Zionists in his thought. Repatriation for Arabs after the establishment of the Jewish state was a major issue for Buber, as Ellis notes. Buber wrote to Ben-Gurion reminding him of the fate of the Jews in Germany (ibid.: 137). Buber chose the 'broken middle-path' in Ellis's view. Buber, Arendt, Magnes and others were dissidents in Zion who were sidelined. Except Hannah Arendt, Buber and Magnes were committed Zionists of liberal order and perhaps in the shadows of their conscious minds, they dreamed of Palestinians haunting the collective psyche of Israel as a nation state. Had their cry, warnings and criticism been heeded by the Zionists, the situation, even though a comprising one, would have been far different than what it is today when Israel has transformed itself as a nation into a killing industry and a war machine.

One dreams more of the fear of the other and enemies rather than dreaming of oneself and one's own friends. Israel has colonized the whole of Palestine, made its spaces habitable for Jews all around the world, but the landscapes of the mind of those who believed that they have returned to their promised national home has been intruded by the Palestinians: Shot and Reverse (a technique invented by Jean Luc Godard to explain repetitions). As Jean Luc Godard in *Notre Musique* explains, 'In 1948 Israel got into the water towards their promised land, Palestinians get into the water to drown... The Jewish people become fiction and the Palestinian people become the documentary.' It is this documentary that haunts fictionalized spaces of the Jewish State.

TWO

MEMORY, GEOGRAPHY, RIFT

I love numbers, but I guess numbers have been reduced to certain meanings let alone human beings. As for geography, it is haunting the texts of the Palestinian literature. [...] In the present fragmentation of space in the geography of Palestine, geography becomes one's own room.

—Adania Shibli

Identity- who we are, where we come from, what we are- is difficult to maintain in exile... We are the 'other', an opposite, a flaw in the geometry of resettlement, an exodus.

—Edward W. Said

In Search of an Inventory

Despite the contributions of the doyen of the Postcolonial Studies, late Edward Said, Palestinian people's struggle and their narratives against the Zionist colonization has been underrepresented in the discourses on colonialism (Moore 2013; Moore-Gilbert 1997). As Edward Said puts it, one of the functions of imperialism and the ruling class has been, 'the power to narrate, or to block other narratives from forming and emerging', and that 'is very important to culture and imperialism and constitutes one of the main connections between them' (Said 1993: xiii). The blocking of narratives and not allowing others to speak has been the hallmark of Zionism, inherited from imperialism.

The same concern is echoed by Jacqueline Rose while talking about Israel's famous novelist Amos Oz whose works have not only been translated into other languages but have become a part of the English literary culture. Rose asks, 'So, who passes into English? Who decides? And at whose expense?' Rose then further argues, 'it's not the political content of his writing that makes Oz controversial. It's his standing. Oz, we might say, straddles two political boundaries'. One, that of the contestation between Israel/Palestine, and other, the 'historical baggage' that Zionism inherits from the English culture (Rose 1996: 22). As Norbert Bugeja (2012: 78) points, 'why has Oz enjoyed such a widespread circulation across the Euro-Atlantic for the past forty odd years, whereas Emile Habibi's, Sahr Khalife's, and Ghassan Kanafani's works, which emerge from the same geo-political problematic as Oz's have, in comparison, languished in the shadows of academia and general 'readership for almost that period?' Within twenty years of its establishment, a prominent Israeli literary figure, Y.S Agnon received the Nobel Prize in Literature while on the other hand writers, poets and critics like Edward Said, Mahmoud Darwish and others could not be heard by the same Norwegian institution. The popular cultural institutions deny the existence of the Palestinians. It happened in the case of a film, *Divine Intervention* by Elia Suleiman, which was submitted to the Academy for the Oscar nomination but they 'refused it, saying there's no country called Palestine' (Edward Said and David Barsamian 2003: 188).

Despite the blockade of Palestinian narratives, Palestinian writers, academics, playwrights, painters, filmmakers and novelists have come up strongly with their words, stories of sufferings, displacements, exile, torture and victimization by the Israeli settler-colonial state. Palestinians living in exile or in continued occupation by Israel have raised their voices in the form of writing memoirs, autobiography, novels, short stories and so on. A number of memoirs have been written especially after Edward Said's memoir *Out of Place.* Raja Shehadeh's three memoirs, *Palestinian Walks: Notes on a Vanishing Landscape*, *Strangers in the House: Coming of Age in the Occupied Palestine* and *A Rift in Time: Travels with my Ottoman Uncle*, Mourid Barghouti's *I Saw Ramallah* and *I was Born There, I was Born Here*, Mahmoud Darwish's *Memory for Forgetfulness*, *In the Presence of Absence* and *The Journal of an Ordinary Grief*, Hanan Ashrawi's *This Side of Peace*, Ghada Karmi's *In Search of Fatima*, Sari Nusseibeh's *Once Upon a Country: A Palestinian Life*, Hala Sakakini's *Jerusalem and I: A Personal Record*, Ibtisam Barakat's *Tasting the Sky: A Palestinian Childhood*, Mitri Raheb's *I am a Palestinian Christian* are the painful 'inventory' of memoirs from all the walks of the Palestinian life expelled from the history by the Zionist colonization since 1948. The titles of these memoirs suggest how geography and memory are intertwined. These memoirs challenge the imperial, colonial and the Zionist narrative of Palestine as an 'empty' territory waiting for the arrival of the Jewish diaspora. In his essay, *Invention, Memory and Place*, Edward Said, while drawing from Eric Hobsbawm's book, *The Invention of Tradition*, suggests how memory and geography hold 'on the desire for conquest and domination' (Said 2000: 181). 'By inventing an ancient Israeli kingdom', Said writes that the Zionist leaders, scholars, artists and novelists have 'made it impossible for the present day Palestinians to say that their claims to Palestine have any long term validity' (ibid.: 187).

Said was realizing how powerless the Palestinians were against the powerful 'invented' discourse created by Zionism while the Palestinians lacked a coherent and convincing 'narrative story with a beginning, middle and end' (ibid.: 185). The production of the 'inventory is a first necessity' and because the Palestinians as victims of Zionism are 'rarely exposed to public view', narrating their life stories are important (Said 1992: 73). The Palestinian writers after Said have filled the gap which Said as a scholar felt. Especially after the failed Oslo peace process, the Palestinians kept on losing more and more lands and the continued occupation dealt a heavy blow to the everyday Palestinian life. This chapter meanders along Shehadeh's text, *Palestinian Walks: Notes on a Vanishing Landscape* and his other memoirs, essays and writings that verge on the time's hinges and geography's shafts.

Raja Shehadeh has captured the continued loss and occupation of Palestinian geography. Shehadeh's memoir, *Palestinian Walks: Notes on a Vanishing Landscape* is a testament to the erasure of the beautiful landscape by Israel's continued building of illegal settlements in West Bank, vulgar colonization and 'land pornography', to use Shehadeh's own words. *Palestinian Walks* is a journey of seven walks (*sarha*) around the hills of West Ramallah which started in 1978 and finished in 2007.

Navigating on a Water of Origin and Ash

I looked and there was my friend,
His face was formed in stone,
His profile defied the wild weather,
In his nose the wind was muffling
the moaning of the persecuted.
There the exile came to the ground.
Changed to the stone, he lives in his own country.

—Pablo Neruda

Shehadeh's memoir, *Palestinian Walks: Notes on a Vanishing Landscape* deconstructs the whole idea of the Zionist imagination and the colonization of Palestine. Since geography as a discipline became an important tool in the hands of the imperialist power, this field of knowledge was rationalized and legitimized to subdue and colonize the non western world as 'laying claim to an idea and laying claim to a territory' in the words of Edward Said, 'were two sides of the same, essentially constitutive activity, which had the force, the prestige and the authority of the *science*' (Said 1992: 73-74). Shehadeh sets out to counter these narratives of the western imagination of Palestine.

William Mackepiece Thackeray who wrote an account of his journey in his book, *Notes on a Journey from Cornhill to Grand Cairo* gave a description of Palestine as 'a landscape unspeakably ghastly and desolate' (Shehadeh 2008: xiii). Palestine was visited, imagined, mapped and talked about in the writings of the prominent British and American writers and novelists like William Thackeray, George Eliot, Dorothy Richardson, Mark Twain, Herman Melville to name a few. One of the major flaws of the mapmaking and cartography right from its invention was that the footsteps of the people, their culture and everyday life, their stories, living beyond European and American frontiers were consciously not marked because people and their culture beyond their frontiers were 'uncivilized', 'brutal' and so many other adjectives which marked 'us' from 'them'.

Shehadeh in *Palestinian Walks* sets out to deconstruct the distorted imagination through his walks which he calls as *sarha* 'in the hills around Ramallah, in the wadis in the Jerusalem wilderness and through the gorgeous ravines by the dead sea' which started in 1978 and ended in 2007 covering a vast space over a period of twenty seven years (ibid.: xii). Shehadeh begins his note of journey with a lament. In the introduction of the memoir, Shehadeh writes,

> When I began hill walking in Palestine, a quarter of a century ago I was not aware that I was travelling through a vanishing landscape. For centuries the central highland hills of Palestine, which slope on the one side towards the sea and the other towards the desert, had remained relatively unchanged. As I grew up in Ramallah, the land from my city to the northern city of Nablus, might with a small stretch of imagination, have seemed familiar to a contemporary of Christ. Those hills were, I believe, one of the natural treasures of the world (ibid.: xi).

The single story of Zionism which Israel as a state constructs on the basis of the biblical imagination subdues and negates the presence of Palestinians as a people and erases their culture. By laying claim to West Bank and renaming it as 'Judea' and 'Samaria', the state of Israel, since the occupation after 1967 is continuously building settlements, transforming the cultural landscape of Palestine, leading to the exclusion, dispossession, marginalization of the Palestinians by inventing myths, memory coupled with modern machinery. As David Harvey puts it, 'Place constructed in the imagery of homogeneity of beliefs, values, ideals, and persuasions coupled with a strong sense of collective memory and spatially exclusionary rights can be extraordinary players upon the world stage. And if, as is so often argued, a place divided against itself will fall, then the maintenance of that permanence that grounds politics becomes an end in itself, however self-destructive it surely must be' (Harvey 1996: 23).

Palestine because of its ties to theological and historical lineages has been a source of inspiration, imagination, contestation and power among the believers of Christianity, Judaism and Islam. As Shehadeh puts it:

> Palestine has been one of the countries most visited by pilgrims and travelers over the ages. The accounts I have read *do not describe a land familiar to me, but rather a land of these travelers' imaginations*. Palestine has been constantly re-invented, with devastating consequences to its original inhabitants. Whether it was the cartographers preparing maps or the travelers describing the landscape in the extensive travel literature, what *mattered was not the land and its inhabitants as they actually were but the confirmation of the viewer's or reader's religious or political beliefs* [Emphasis added] (Shehadeh 2008: xii).

As Henri Lefebvre argues, the social construction and the 'silencing and manipulation of the users of the space' by the power of imagination, construction of beliefs, negating and subduing the lived experiences of the people living through generations in a particular 'place of social space as a whole is usurped by a part of that space endowed with an illusory special status- namely, the part which is concerned with writing and imagery, underpinned by the written text (journalism, literature), and broadcast by the media; a part, in short, that amounts to abstraction wielding awesome reductionistic forces vis-à-vis 'lived' experience (Lefebvre 1991: 52). Further down the line Shehadeh quotes Mark Twain who went on a 'pleasure trip' aboard *Quaker City* on 8th June 1867 from New York's Wall Street on a expedition to Europe and the Holy Land and the description of his journey was recollected by Twain in his book, *The Innocents Abroad or The New Pilgrims Progress,* published in 1869. Once Twain landed in Palestine, he wrote

> Palestine sits in sackcloth and ashes. Over it broods the spell of a curse that has withered its fields and fettered its energies... Nazareth is forlorn... Jericho the accursed... Bethlehem and Bethany, in their poverty and humiliation... Jerusalem has lost its ancient grandeur. Palestine is desolate and unlovely. And why should it be otherwise? Can the curse of a deity, beautify a land? Palestine is no more of this workday world. It is sacred to poetry and tradition- It is dream-land (Shehadeh 2008: xiii).

For Shehadeh, the distorted description and the representation of Palestine is not the true picture of Palestine as opposed to his 'relationship to the land' where he has 'always lived, as immediate and not experienced through the veil of words written about it, often replete with distortions' (ibid.: xiii). The landscape, its culture, its people, its history through generations, its stories of everyday life belonged to the Palestinians but the master craftsmen, cartographers and storytellers were either Europeans or the Americans in origin. As Jean Paul Sartre in his introduction to Frantz Fanon's text, *Wretched of the Earth,* writes, 'the former had the word; the others had the use of it' (Fanon 2001: 7). The brutality and the molestation of the Palestinian landscape and its culture is what irks Shehadeh. The words printed on a piece of paper have taken away the voices of the Palestinians. In the words of Edward Said, 'Imperialism and Zionism has monopolized the entire system of representation' (Said 1993: 27). Shehadeh writes about the Palestinians as the very thing that renders 'the landscape "biblical", its traditional inhabitation and cultivation in terraces, olive orchards, the stone building and the presence of livestock is produced by the Palestinians, whom the Jewish settlers came to replace. And yet, the very people who cultivate the "green olive orchards" and render the landscape biblical are themselves excluded from the panorama. The Palestinians are there to produce the scenery and then disappear... In the process history, mine and that of my people is distorted and twisted' (Shehadeh 2008: xiv-xiv).

Since 1967, successive Israeli governments planned to populate West Bank with settlements. The father and the architect of settlement building in West Bank, Ariel Sharon, 'played a major role, saw the territorialities of the occupied territories as "elastic" and up for grabs' (Weizman 2007: 88). For Shehadeh when he heard about all these plans of building the settlements illegally in the occupied West Bank, he felt, he had 'contracted a terminal disease' (Shehadeh 2008: xvi). The manner in which building of the settlements and creating 'facts on the ground' is connected to the brutal imagination of Zionism and occupation leaves no ground for the Palestinians. In a speech in the Israeli Knesset, Menachem Begin in May, 1982 said, 'Settlements... scores, almost one hundred years ago, in areas of the land of Israel populated by Arabs and sometimes solely by Arabs- was it moral or immoral; permitted or forbidden? One of the two. If it was moral then settlement near Nablus is moral—There is no third way' (Auerbach 2013). The settlements for Israel as Eyal Weizman (2007: 8) writes, 'is understood by the Israeli public' as a 'national-messianic right'. It has been inducted into the core of Zionist philosophy by claiming that Israel has the 'moral' legitimacy to build settlements in the occupied territories even if it contravenes the International law and the Fourth Geneva Convention. Following the defense minister, Ariel Sharon's statement, 'we are going to leave an entirely different map of the country that it will be impossible to ignore', the Israeli Prime Minister Menachem Begin said, 'settlement [in the occupied areas] is the soul of Zionism' (Shehadeh 2008: 56). Oslo Accords failed to stop the burgeoning of the settlements in the occupied territories of the West Bank. Shehadeh laments how Palestinian leaders like Arafat and Mahmoud Abbas were blind to the combined forces of Israeli power with its legal institutions which take away the Palestinian lands under the pretext of a labyrinth of laws which Israel invents to deny Palestinians access to their own lands. Arafat's main aim was 'to secure recognition for the PLO' from Israel and the United States (ibid.: 101). Since the Oslo Accords were signed, the building of the settlements in the occupied areas doubled. Shehadeh notes,

> As we drove down to Jericho we passed the fledgling new settlements of Mitzpe Jericho. The language of conquest was writ large over the hills, over the wilderness, in every corner of the land. Everything signaled our defeat- from the earlier rows of settler apartment blocks piled over the dry pink hills forming the city of Maaleh Adumin to this latest settlement venture in the wilderness... The countryside I grew up in was being transformed [...] to make the 'desert' bloom with concrete and neon lights. Vast areas of my beloved country were being fenced to become off limits to us (ibid.: 112-114).

Shehadeh is witness to these changes while the land under the Palestinian control 'was slipping' beneath their feet 'as the Dead Sea was receding from its salty shores' (ibid.: 117). Shehadeh laments, 'Oslo Agreements buried my truth' (ibid.: 123).

Archiving the Stones, Earth, Water and Stories

At the graveside of Emily Habiby, the renowned Palestinian poet, novelist, the epitaph reads as: *I Stayed in Haifa*. On the cover page of his memoir, *The Third Way* (1982), Raja Shehadeh wrote, 'Between mute submission and blind hate. I chose the third way. I chose *Sumud*. *Sumud* is not an ordinary word for the Palestinians; it has rather entered into the vocabulary of the resistance politics in the Palestinian context. *Sumud* means 'steadfastness' or to 'stay put' which is 'the art of hanging on at all costs and against all odds, a mental and spiritual state of being that thousands of Palestinians have learned is not easy to master' (Audeh 1983: 77). For the Palestinians *Sumud* is an art of resistance to Zionist colonization very much like that of the everyday unorganized resistance by peasants described by James Scott in *Weapons of the Weak: Everyday Forms of Peasant Resistance* (1985). The tools of resistance or 'weapons of the weak' as Scott views are foot-dragging, evasion, false compliance, pilfering, feigned ignorance, slander and sabotage. In the case of the Palestinians, the force of the Zionist colonization is more fierce than that of the peasants described by James Scott. Through his *sarha,* Shehadeh is involved in a process of archiving the Palestinian space and time as well as the stories of people who passed through these landscapes which are being continuously erased by the power of heavy bulldozers and other machinery combined with a force of biblical imagination. The fact that for Shehadeh it took almost twenty seven years for seven walks along the *wadis* and hills, signify how painful the occupation has been for the ordinary Palestinians. Shehadeh while lamenting and grieving on the erasure of the landscape, writes, 'the biography of these hills is in many ways my own, the victories and the failures of the struggle to save this land also mine. But the persistent pain at the failure of that struggle would in time be shared by Arabs, Jews and the lovers of nature anywhere in the world. All would grieve, as I have at the continuing destruction of an exquisitely beautiful place' (Shehadeh 2008: 1).

In the process of taking walks or *sarha,* Shehadeh writes a biography of the hills which he thinks would in time be erased as a result of the brutal colonization by the Israeli state. Remembering the legacy of Abu Ameen, cousin of Shehadeh's grandfather, Judge Saleem, Shehadeh inherits this legacy of walking in Palestinian style. Shehadeh writes, 'To go on a *sarha* was to roam freely, at will, without restraint. The verb form of the word means to let the cattle out to pasture early in the morning, leaving them to wander and graze at liberty. The commonly used noun *sarha* is a colloquial corruption of the classical word. A man going on a *sarha* wanders aimlessly, not restricted by time and place, going where his spirits take him to nourish his soul and rejuvenate himself... Going on a *sarha* implies letting go. It is a drug-free high, Palestinian style' (ibid.: 2). Along with his *sarha,* Shehadeh takes the reader on *sarha* as well. He invites the reader to go on an imaginary *sarha* along with him. 'Each *sarha* is in the form of a walk that I invite the reader to take with me. I hope by describing what can be seen, heard and smelled in the hills, to allow the reader to enjoy the unique experience of a *sarha* in Palestine' (ibid.: 2). 'To walk across a landscape with any degree of awareness,' as Massey (2008) suggests, 'is to pick your way across the locations of a host of unfinished trajectories. Their unfinished addresses of our today'. Walking is a process of 'enunciation' (De Certeau 1984). 'To walk is to lack a place', a process signifying absence as De Certeau suggests, 'an indefinite process of being absent and in search of a proper' (De Certeau 1984: 103). Places where people live are not 'containers' but 'the presence of diverse absences' (ibid.: 108). Places are defined and 'composed by a series of displacements', 'fragmentary and inward turning histories, pasts that others are not allowed to read, accumulated times that can be unfolded but like stories held in reserve' (ibid.: 108). Literally by going through Shehadeh's memoir I was filled with shame. What do I know about the landscape of my own university which is situated on a range of Aravali hills? What do I know about the stories about these hills? What do I know about the geography of a university apart from its politics and daily gossips and random walks with friends on a hilltop? Geography plays no part in university's thinking and philosophico-political discourses today. One of the reasons for the decline of universities today is that geography of the mind is held hostage.

Sarha for Shehadeh is not only an ordinary walk but a resistance to Israeli occupation, continuously stopping him from walking freely on a landscape to which he belongs. The irony of occupation is that as Shehadeh writes, it is far easier for a person from Gaza to visit China but a merely a 45 minute journey to Ramallah_is a distant dream (Shehadeh 2008: xvii). *Sarha* in Palestine is a dream nowadays as a result of occupation and dividing the landscape in several Bantustans like labyrinth of settlements, checkpoints, blockades, zoning, 'enclaving' and 'exclaving', a separation wall so high that it would put the Berlin wall to shame. Shehadeh's first *sarha* after his return to Ramallah in 1978 led him to the path where he 'stumbled, quite by accident, upon the legendary Harrasha of Abu Ameen, deep in the hills of Palestine' (ibid.: 7). On his way to the hills he found a 'well preserved *qasr*,' a castle and reminded him of his grandfather and Abu Ameen when they camped in one of those similar structures on their way to *sarha*. Overwhelmed by the 'exploding beauty and colour' of the earth, Shehadeh shouted 'S-A-R-H-A!' He felt he was, 'breaking the silence of the past, a silence that has enveloped this place for a long time' (ibid.: 9). Shehadeh quotes Herman Melville, the famous American novelist and the author of Moby Dick who treaded the same path and described it as 'Whitish mildew pervading whole tracts of landscape - bleached-leprosy-encrustations of curses-old cheese-bones of rocks... all Judea seems to have been accumulations of this rubbish' (ibid.: 10). The distortion of the imagination can be seen when a Palestinian who has lived and experienced the same landscape as Shehadeh describes it and feels as though he could 'sit all day next to this *qasr*' and feast his 'eyes on this wonderful creation' (ibid.: 10).

The identities and dignity of the variegated people, their culture and their landscape distorted by naming, framing and the power of imagination leading to a distorted image has been exposed in a critical study of geographical imagination in *Orientalism* by Edward Said. Each *sarha* Shehadeh takes across the landscape of Palestine is replete with stories associated with space across time. It seems as if the rocks, the trees, the bushes, the *qasr*, have induced Shehadeh to go into a conversation about the stories and the footsteps of the landscape. While treading the fertile plain of Marj Ibn A'mr (Jazreel valley) 'which stretches below the Carmel mountains to Jenin in the West Bank and breathtaking hills of Galilee', Shehadeh's imagination goes back to the battles, pathways of traders and pilgrims. 'This was the place where pitched battles were fought before the sixteenth century, leaving the remainders and ruins of the fortifications and castles of various invaders' (ibid.: 6). Crossing Wadi Matar (rain), Shehadeh comes across a number of abandoned *qasrs* and starts thinking who might have been the inhabitants of these *qasrs.* Shehadeh talks about meeting Fareed, an inhabitant of Ramallah who now lives as a member of the diasporic community in Washington D.C.; he recalls that 'his strongest memory of growing up in Ramallah was pressed toes cramped in tight shoes' (ibid.: 13). Further down the line Shehadeh while examining an abandoned *qasr* imagined about a family who had been the owner of this abandoned *qasr:*

> I could imagine him sitting by this window, as I was doing, and surveying his possessions. Perhaps he had a number of children whom he observed from and hurled orders at : 'You, Muneer, pick up those stones over there and plough the land around that plum tree.' 'You, Fareed, water that aurbegine plant over there.'... It was as though in this *qasr* time was petrified into an eternal present, making it possible for me to reconnect with my dead ancestors through this architectural wonder (ibid.: 14).

For Shehadeh 'time was petrified into an eternal present' which allows him to build a thread of connection with his 'dead ancestors through this architectural wonder' (ibid.:15). Examining an 'oddly placed stone', scraping it, which later turned out be a carved sitting chair, imagining it to be an *a'rsh* (throne) of an anonymous person, Shehadeh delves into the past and recalls that as a child he heard of Abu Ameen, his grandfather's cousin having an *a'rsh* next to his *qasr.* 'Could this be it? Could this be Harrasha where Abu Ameen and my grandfather Saleem used to go for their *sarha*?', asks Shehadeh (ibid.: 17). Abu Ameen turns out be a romantic who married a woman named Zariefeh and took her to honeymoon in his newly bought property, built a *qasr,* spent half of the year at home and remaining half at the hills.

Abu Ameen was not aware of what was going to befall on his future generations after the creation of the state of Israel and further colonization and occupation of West Bank.

> Abu Ameen was able to look out on the hills that remained unchanged ... He could not have been aware how fortunate he was to have security and the comfort of seeing the same unaltered view of the hills... But throughout my life I had the misfortune of witnessing their constant transformation. I first learned the Israeli government's settlement plans ... one hilltop after the other was claimed as more and more Jewish settlements were established. Then the settlements were joined with each other to form 'settlement blocks'. Roads were built between these clusters and ever expanding areas of land around them were reserved for their future growth, depriving more villages of the agricultural land they depended upon for their livelihood. Thus one block of settlements was created north of Ramallah, another to the east and many more to the south. And between the blocks to the east smaller

> settlements called outposts began to crop up so that when I looked at night towards the north I saw a continuous stretch of settlements and roads that were creating a noose around Ramallah ... complicating our lives immeasurably and causing yet another damage to our beautiful landscape (ibid.: 32-33).

Shehadeh is being witness to the destruction caused to the landscape, its trajectory and stories through a process beautifully captured by Eyal Weizman as, 'elastic geography' and 'biblical archaeology'. As Doreen Massey argues, 'space is a dimension of 'multiplicity', 'contemporaneous existence of a plurality of trajectories, radical simultaneity, of trajectories; a simultaneity of stories so far' (Massey 2005: 8-14). Space is always open ended and it's not a flat surface or a 'container', as Massey suggests the space is imbued with 'coevalness of stories and voices.' Shehadeh's Ramallah hills, abandoned *qasrs* and *a'rsh* and the places wherever he goes around echoes the stories of the past which enable him to connect with the present. As Lefebvre argues, 'time is inscribed in space' (Lefebvre 1991: 95) as different patches of colours in a woven carpet.

Zionism's idea of going back into space-time to construct, frame and name the spaces in the biblical imagination is to enclose the space, thereby bringing both space and time to halt, is depriving the Palestinians of their landscape connected to their stories of everyday life which, in turn, is connected to memory. As Massey puts it, 'you can't go back in space-time. To think that you can is to deprive others of their independent stories' (Massey 2005: 125). The whole idea of the Zionist policy is to erase the landscape along with the history, trajectory, stories and voices of the Palestinians. The idea of the Zionist policy of taking over the hilltops thereby affirming control over the surface of the earth while its archaeology is involved in digging deep to trace the roots of a Biblical land selectively in Bronze age which refers to 'Cananite' period and Iron age which refers to the 'Israelite period' erases the history of the rest of the layers connected to a Palestinian presence or an Arab presence. The process of subduing and rendering mute the multiplicity and the stories of the other are done through a political and tactical use of archaeology. As Colin Renfrew and Paul Bahn write,

> Having established on much of a surface of unfamiliar Palestine, Zionism continued its vertical quest for the Promised Land downwards... The national role assigned to archeology was to remove the visible layer and expose the ancient Israelite landscape and with it the proof of Jewish ownership (Weizman 2007: 39).

Eyal Weizman beautifully captures the politics of archaeology in erasing Islamic cultural pasts. Weizman writes,

> A few meters below the surface, a palimpsest of 5,000 year-old debris, a vertical chronological stack of cultures of lives, narratives of war and destruction, has been compressed by soil and stone. Israeli Biblical archaeologists were interested in the deeper levels of Bronze and iron ages, which generally cover the period and time mentioned in the more recent religious interpretations of the Mishna. The upper layers of the Muslim and Ottoman periods were marginalized in digs and museums often dismissed as representations of a stagnant period, discarded as too new or simply left alone to rot and crumble (Weizman 2007: 40).

As Said (1993: 6) argues that across the geographical terrain, 'empty uninhabited spaces virtually do not exist'. Spaces do have their histories, stories, trajectories, voices, as argued by Massey and to which Said refers as 'overlapping territories, intertwined histories'. The imperial and the Zionist culture of imagining and constructing a single story of a space devoid of people, voices and history in a quest for 'making the desert bloom' is a politically motivated invention and construction with appalling consequences befalling on Palestinians as a people. The Zionist narrative in the process created 'facts on the ground', linking archaeology to mythology to produce a homogenous Jewish identity and 'erase the question of "Palestine" from the history of Israeli state and society, which had become, quite simply, the nation-state of and for the Jewish people' (Abu El-Haj 2001: 5). As Harvey suggests, cultural-politics combined with political-economic power, 'intertwine in the social processes of place construction' (Harvey 1996: 320). The state and its institutions of power imply a 'certain aestheticization of politics' as Harvey suggests, combined with the 'appeal to the mythology of a place and person' to achieve its nationalistic goals and the 'rhetoric of national liberation movements... imposed through imperialism and colonialism, of manifest destiny, racial or cultural supremacy, paternalism (white man's burden for example), and doctrines of national superiority' (Harvey 1990: 209).

By creating 'facts on the ground', the state of Israel in the process of colonizing Palestine is robbing Shehadeh of his own history, memories, and the story of his Ottoman past where his great-great uncle Najib Nassar was on the run after being sought by the Ottoman authorities. Shehadeh paints the whole picture and traces the trajectory of his uncle's route while escaping the Ottoman authorities in another memoir, *A Rift in Time: Travels with my Ottoman Uncle*. Shehadeh writes,

> To locate the places where Najib found refuge during his long escape from the Ottoman police, I first used a map made by the Israeli Survey Department. But I soon discovered that, in the course of creating a new country over the ruins of the old, Israel has renamed almost every hill, spring and wadi in Palestine, striking from the map names and often habitations that had been there for centuries (Shehadeh 2010: 3).

Failing to trace the escape route through the Israeli map, Shehadeh was able to locate the places from a 1933 map which he procured from the National Library of Scotland in Edinburg. Shehadeh further writes,

> The quest for Najib – the details of his life and the route of his great escape- that consumed me for the next thirteen years was not an easy one. Most of the Palestine's history, together with that of its people, is buried deep in the ground. To reconstruct the journey of my great-great uncle I could not visit any of the houses where he and his family had lived in Haifa, his point of departure. This mixed community of Arabs and Jews has become an Israeli city, with most of its former Palestinian inhabitants scattered through the world. Najib died on 30 March, 1948, just months before the Nakba (catastrophe), the mass expulsion and dispossessions of the Arabs of Palestine in 1948... His wife, siblings, and every one of our common relatives were forced out of Haifa, losing all their property... Furnitures, books, manuscripts, memorabilia, family photographs, heirlooms...Everything that belonged to them, everything that told their individual stories, was either stolen or seized and deposited in Israeli archives for use by Israeli researchers seeking to understand the history and character of the Arabs whom they were colonizing (ibid.: 4-5).

Shehadeh's parents and his forefathers were born and raised in Jaffa, a port city which is now a part of the Jewish State of Israel. Its inhabitants were forced to leave Jaffa as a result of the 'ethnic cleansing of Palestine'. It was here the Zionist militia, the Stern Gang, carrying a truck of oranges entered into the centre of the town and left it to explode. On 22 April 1948, as Shehadeh writes, Jaffa fell to the Zionist forces. Thinking that Shehadeh's parents will return to Jaffa after the UN Partition plan, he writes in *Strangers in the House*, 'two weeks stretched into forever' (Shehadeh 2010a: 5). Shehadeh could only imagine about Jaffa through the stories of his parents and grandmother. For a long time as a child lost in the imagination of a city which fell, he writes,

> Across the horizon in the beautiful city of which I heard about and yearned to see... hostage to memories, perceptions, and attitudes of the others that I cannot abandon. My sense of place was not mine... My life was shaped by the contrast between meagerness of life in Ramallah and the opulence of life in the city across the hills. *There were daily reminders of that cataclysmic fall from grace* and I could count on my grandmother always to point them out. One was the son of Issa passing by our house pushing a cart with a few objects for sale: an old bottle, a tin can, a few articles of clothing, and an old kerosene stove called a Primus [Emphasis added] (ibid.: 1-9).

Jaffa was home to Shehadeh's ancestors where his father was an acclaimed lawyer and later served in the Jordanian foreign ministry. As a result of the 'ethnic cleansing' and Plan Dalet, Ilan Pappé observed in his book, *The Ethnic Cleansing of Palestine*, that Jaffa was the last of the Palestinian territories which fell to Zionist forces on 13th May. A massive force of '5000 Irgun and Haganah troops attacked the city' and laid a three week siege to the city and in defense of Jaffa there were only '1500 volunteers' (Pappé 2006: 102-103). One of the battalions called Jaffa Brigade which was to be headed by an Iraqi commander, Abdel Wahab, consisted of, as Shehadeh writes, 'a baker, the blacksmith, a farmer and the man who sold newspapers' to defend it. The balance of force was obviously in favour of Israel, its units trained and assisted by the British colonial forces against which the Arabs had no chance. The city and its houses were 'dynamited with people still in them' (Pappé 2006: 75) and out of 24 villages and 17 mosques in Jaffa as Pappé writes, 'today one mosque survives but none of the villages is left standing' (ibid.: 102). After the victory of the Zionist forces and the fall of the city, its population of '50, 000 was expelled with the "help" of British mediation' (ibid.: 103). Pappé describes the horrific scene of their flight in the northern harbor of Haifa. He writes, 'people were literally pushed in to the sea when the crowds tried to board the far-too-small fishing boats that would take them to Gaza, while Zionist troops shot over their heads to hasten their expulsion' (ibid.: 103). In *Strangers in the House,* Shehadeh describes about the visit to Jaffa years after the al-Nakba, 1948 when Shehadeh's father's old friend David Rosenblum came to see him after 1967 occupation of the West Bank and asked him 'if he could do anything', Shehadeh's father had only one wish: to see Jaffa again. On his father's arrival in Jaffa at Nuzha street, at his mother-in-law's house, he stood at the entrance gate and saw that 'it was just as he left it, only now the paint was peeling' (Shehadeh 2010a: 59). A city in ruins, its population expelled, never to return, Shehadeh writes, 'Ghosts from the past do not freeze in time: their gardens continue to grow, their walls peel from the ravages of nature and neglect' (ibid.: 59). David Rosenblum took Shehadeh's father to see the Jaffa seashore at sunset, 'two men of the same age and height, a Palestinian and a Jew, stood side by side in the twilight of a ruined city' (ibid.: 61). Here the past is fused with the present to evoke a sense of place that is lost, to which Jacqueline Rose refers to as 'the baggage of the mind' and 'nothing... is simply left behind' (Rose: 2007: 41). Zionism's construction of a homogenous space and its understanding of space as a 'flat surface,' as a 'container' where Jews from diaspora can come and fill this 'container' obscures the fact that a homogenous Jewish identity constructed on the basis of an organized and institutionalized memory of a past and nostalgia has forced the Palestinians to leave and live as exiles both internal and external. As Doreen Massey argues, the articulation of a nostalgic past in space and time 'robs other of their histories' (Massey 2005: 124).

Zionism's going back into space-time has robbed Palestinians of their own past and 'ongoing independent stories', to use Doreen Massey's words (ibid.: 125). 'This is a nation which desires its potential citizens- exiled, diaspora Jewry-to come home, with as much fervor', as Jacqueline Rose, a prominent psychoanalyst, writes, 'as it banishes the former occupants of its land from their own dream of statehood' (Rose 1996: 2). Rose writes further, 'Displacing the Palestinians, it then produced on the spot a new people without statehood not just by oversight or brutal self- realizing intention, but as if it had symptomatically to engender within its own boundaries the founding conditions from which it had fled' (ibid.: 13). Shehadeh's memory of experienced, lived places is not dictated by mythical construction as opposed to Zionism's construction of a collective memory. As Mourid Barghouti said, 'our song is not for some sacred thing of the past but for our current self-respect that is violated anew everyday' (Barghouti 2003: 7). Contrary to the imaginations of Shehadeh and Barghouti, Amos Oz's narrative of the same space is framed in a messianic tone when he writes, 'we would build ourselves a land a thousand times as beautiful here' (Rose 1996: 24). Oz's imagination obscures, hides, negates a very fundamental fact about space; the existence of Palestinians, their history and stories. 'Emptied of its history, the land is packed with appropriating mythological intent' (ibid.: 24). As Shehadeh himself writes,

> Europe and later Zionism, has endeavoured to rescue the historical significance of the region in its search for ancient Israel: a search for its own cultural roots which in the process has silenced Palestinian history and relegated it to prehistory, paving the way for the modern state of Israel to take control not only of the land but also of Palestinian time and space (Shehadeh 2008: 47).

Shehadeh's *sarha* which he takes in the present tense sense of time continuously fuses with the past and the places where he goes for *sarha* is coupled with an imaginary *sarha* of a past filled with anecdotes, history, people, both of his own past and of the past of his own community. For Shehadeh, heroism lies in the determination of the Palestinian people to 'stay put', and 'not in our acts of daring or even in military operations' (Shehadeh 2010a: 141). As Moore argues, 'resistance in this text is conceived in at least two chronotopic modes. A shift explicitly registered from *sarha* to *sumoud*' (Moore 2013: 37). Shehadeh in the process is also invoking the past to 'stay put' against the Zionist occupation. Both the *sarhas,* the physical walks in the hills and the imaginary *sarha* of history, memories and stories are intertwined and is engaged in *sumoud.* Against the slogan of Menachem Begin, 'There is no third way', Shehadeh chose his own 'third way', that of resistance through *Sumud.*

Coming to Terms with the Present: Geographical Conditions

The Oslo Accords that was signed between Israel and the PLO did not lead to the self determination of the Palestinian people. Since the signing of the Oslo Accords the building of the settlements in the West Bank heightened to the degree that Shehadeh has lost hope in the peace process. Since his involvement in the legal struggle to contain further Israeli colonization of Palestine, he views that the PLO was not concerned about the legal ramifications of the peace process. He hoped that the 'settlements would not be permanent' (Shehadeh 2008: 123). 'The legal battles waged for years' which gave a meaning to Shehadeh's life as he writes, 'were not recognized by the leadership' (ibid.:124). The signing of the Oslo Accords terminated and put an end to Shehadeh's 'narrative' and he felt, 'my bubble, my illusion was burst' (ibid.: 124). He is aware of the looming disaster which is going to befall on this landscape. People find meaning of their lives in resistance to the occupation and in terms of the Palestinians, their existential meaning of life is forged through resistance where people contribute in a variety of ways to resist colonization. For Shehadeh it was the law through which he was contesting the occupation. 'What had framed my existence and given it a heightened sense of purpose was my resistance to the occupation, my work for justice' (ibid.: 129). As a part of the delegation to the Oslo Accords he knew that the terms of the agreement were drafted by Israeli lawyers who were experts in the field. One of the reasons Shehadeh joined the delegation was because he thought he could be of help to the PLO in understanding Israeli tactics and legal maneuvers.

The vision to challenge the occupation through law encouraged Shehadeh to establish his own organization called *Al-Haq* in 1978 which produced a series of documents and exposed Israeli land confiscations, building of settlements, checkpoints, roads, diverting key resources like water for the Israeli settlers while leaving the Palestinians to subsist on a bare minimum. It was his commitment to justice, freedom and democracy that allowed Shehadeh to rebel against his father who was under continuous Israeli pressure to dissuade Shehadeh from continuing his work against occupation and 'accept the way things are' (Shehadeh 2010a: 182). The dispute between father and son is documented in Shehadeh's memoir, *Strangers in the House.* Shehadeh writes, 'My strong convictions prevented me from accepting my father's position. I looked at his generation as the defeated one... My father's attitude came partly from concern for my well being and partly from pride. He could not allow me to do what he had always done' (ibid.: 182-183). Despite all of the challenges Shehadeh continued to document illegal practices of Israeli torture, land confiscations, house demolitions, abuse of human rights, etc. Shehadeh documents the two confrontations on his walk along the hills: one, between him and the settler and the other between two young Palestinians. After a heated discussion with the settler, both settled for smoking *nergila* (joint). Shehadeh writes, 'I was fully aware of the looming tragedies and war that lay ahead for both of us, Palestinian Arab and Israeli Jew. But for now he and I could sit together, for a respite, for a smoke, joined temporarily for the mutual love of our land' (Shehadeh 2008: 203). The experience of facing two Palestinian boys wearing *kuffieh,* masked as shepherd, was worse than meeting the settler. 'Shaken' by the encounter, Shehadeh's memoir ends with a sad note. He decided that he would not be coming to those hills anymore. He writes,

> As I stood in the ruins of one of my favourite places in the valley ... I felt that the hills were not mine anymore... They have become a dangerous place where I do not feel safe... I bid this valley farewell. I would not be coming here for a long time. Perhaps not before this damned conflict with Israel with all its nasty consequences ends, if this should happen in my lifetime (ibid. 214-215).

Shehadeh's quest for justice and a 'just' solution for the Palestinian question is 'buried' by the Oslo Accords. 'Nothing can be done to change the past but I knew I had to come to terms with the present. The truth was that we had been defeated. We had lost' (ibid.: 118). Gilbert Moore identifies Shehadeh's dilemma of 'coming to terms with the present' as 'the critique of the notion of singular *presence*' (Moore 2013: 41). Moore while taking cue from Edward Said, Judith Butler and Shehadeh's own memoir, *A Rift in Time: Travels With My Ottoman Uncle,* calls for a 'therapeutic teleology' where the two communities could identify with each other's historical and geographical pain and make way for a '*democracy to come*,' to use Jacques Derrida's phrase.

Jacqueline Rose in her essay on Israel/Palestine question argues how the trauma and suffering of the Jews in holocaust is being transferred from Jews to Palestinians which she refers to as 'transgenerational haunting', while referring to David Grossman and Raja Shehadeh. In Shehadeh's *Third Way,* he dreams that he is a 'victim of the victims of the Nazis ... I am more aware of the concentration camps, think about them more and more and dream about them more than the average Israeli does' (Shehadeh 1982: 64 quoted in Rose 1996: 31). Rose points out to the 'historical pain' shifting across the geographical terrain of the mind. However, the 'transgenerational haunting' is not restricted to Shehadeh's writing alone. It is also reflected in Sari Nusseibeh's memoir, *Once Upon a Country: A Palestinian Life* and in other writings by Palestinian people. Nusseibeh writes,

> One day my older sister Saedah, thirteen at the time, fell into an uncontrollable fit of tears. She had brought home from school a copy of *The Diary of Anne Frank.* She cried and cried in anguished identification with this Jewish child hidden in an annex, terrified at being found out by killers of her people. It was paradoxical identification for the daughter of a mother who had suffered so much at the hands of the Zionists. But without a word, my mother gently wiped Saedah's tears away, and furtively wiped her own (Nussiebeh 2007: 66-67).

Rose's 'transgenerational haunting' which Nussiebeh addresses as 'paradoxical identification' is now experienced by the Palestinians in their everyday life as is evident from Shehadeh's and Nussiebeh's memoirs. The geopolitical shifting of pain from Europe to Palestine identified by the Palestinians is the recognition of the Jewish experience. This 'paradoxical identification' and transmission of 'historical pain' experienced by both Israelis and Palestinians has to pave a way for a democratic state where the right of return of the Palestinians will be recognized by the democracy loving Jewish people. Shehadeh addresses this question through a secular and an open interpretation of geography. As suggested by Doreen Massey in her brilliant work, *For Space,* for the future to be progressive and for a secular interpretation of culture and space, the space has to be 'open'. Shehadeh delves into the landscape of the past and comes out with an interpretation of geography which identifies its plurality and paves the way for a geographical identification. Taking cue from Edward Said's idea of secular criticism, Doreen Massey's idea of space, Sari Nussiebeh's 'paradoxical identification' and Jacqueline Rose's 'transgenerational haunting', I suggest an idea of geographical identification where both the Palestinians and Israelis as manifested in Shehadeh's writing, identify geography as a trajectory of 'multiple stories' (Massey 2005), multiple histories, 'overlapping territories, intertwined histories' (Said 1993). The negation of a single story of space will allow us to have a secular interpretation of space. As Shehadeh writes in two different texts,

> The diversity of cultures that once thrived here – the Bedouins and the villagers, the marshland farmers and shepherds coming to Palestine from Egypt, Iran, Jordan, Lebanon, Morocco, a mix of Bahais, Christians, Jews and Muslims... I will succeed in imaginatively creating the region as it existed at the time of the Ottoman Empire, when the land was undivided. This will be my way of resisting what Israel has long tried to drill into my head about my place in this ancient land after the fragmentation of our territory... (Shehadeh 2010: 48-49).

And,

> In the twenty-first century the case of Palestine remains one of the last surviving examples of a country usurped by a colonial project exploiting religion to deprive Palestinians of their land. I am convinced that only when these wild contortions of history, religion and international law are challenged will Arabs and Jew come to accept each other, as my father and I were able to do. No strangers will then remain in our house (Shehadeh 2010a: 241).

Edward Said remarks that the 'task at hand' is to come to terms with 'each of the two communities, misled though both may be, is interested in its origins, its history of suffering, its need to survive. To recognize these imperatives, as components of national identity, and to try to reconcile them rather than dismiss them as so much non factual ideology strikes me as the task at hand' (Said 1994: 268). Shehadeh's 'rift in time' addressed through an autobio-geographical incursion into the spatialities and temporalities of being and memory as he hopes may pave a way for a geographical condition of 'dwelling' into each other in Heideggerian sense by recognizing the traces, histories, geographies, and memories of the *other* in the spaces of self and the way back.

THREE

RETURN, PRESENCE, ABSENCE

> Memories of the outside world will never have the same tonality as those of home and, by recalling these memories, we add to our store of dreams; we are never really historians, but always near poets, and our emotion is perhaps nothing but an expression of poetry that was lost.
>
> – Gaston Bachelard

> Everything here is proof of loss and lack. Everything here is a painful reminder of what had once been there. What wounds you most is that there is so close to here.
>
> – Mahmoud Darwish

How can one write about Mourid Barghouti's writings without imagining the accumulation of dust gathered on the pathways of exile and home? The layers of dust hides a scab, a gentle scratch opens a dark country, spreading its pain over white sheets. His writings are long pathways, detours and returns to everyday pleasures and agonies of being and not being, absences and presences, sweet tastes of olives and bitterness of distance that separates his nights from the days. Reading Barghouti's memoirs is like reading Marcel Proust's *In Search of Lost Time*. There is a narrow bridge of pale, breathless night that connects Proust to Barghouti. Such is the agony of the autobiographical subject torn between *here* and *there*. The book clears the haziness in which the landscape is shrouded, and beyond this horizon of landscape lies cure. The malady that subject is, receives treatment from beautiful verses opening like flower buds surrounded by thorns. His memoir *Ra'aytu Ramallah* was originally published in Arabic in 1997. *I Saw Ramallah* as the English translation appeared in 2000 translated by Ahdaf Soueif with a foreword written by Edward Said. Subsequently his other memoir, *I Was Born There, I was Born Here,* a sequel to the first, is an account of the second phase of his journey to Ramallah with his son, Tamim al-Barghouti who sees Palestine for the first time. Barghouti in his own words belongs to the part of the world with 'negated history and a threatened geography' (Barghouti 2008). Barghouti's memoir is an account of a life spent as an exile for thirty years in different parts of the world and a return to his homeland after the tragic Oslo Accords which allowed Barghouti to see his birthplace once again. Edward Said in the preface writes that *I Saw Ramallah* 'is one of the finest existential accounts of Palestinian displacement' (Barghouti 2003: vii). Mourid Barghouti was in Cairo writing his final year undergraduate exams when the 1967 war just broke out. As a result of the war, Israel occupied West Bank which stopped Barghouti from returning to Palestine and forced him to live in exile for thirty years. The 1967 war was a second catastrophe for the Palestinians, the first one being the 1948 *Nakba*. In his own memoir, *Out of Place,* Edward Said writes how he was shattered with the defeat as 'it brought more dislocations' which embodied 'the dislocations that subsumed all other losses' and he 'was no longer the same person after 1967' (Said 1999: 293). To this day, Palestine remains the last colony and Israel, the last colonizer on this earth where peoples, cultures, communities of other nations are enjoying the so-called fruit of 'neoliberalization' and 'globalization'. For the majority of the world, time is on the move or even running while the Palestinians are chained by dislocations, exiles, checkpoints, permits, walls, ghettoization, apartheid, both physical and cultural by Israeli colonization. The world calls Palestinians as the

Naziheen, the displaced ones (Barghouti 2003: 9). Barghouti writes, 'displacement is like death' (ibid.: 3) and 'at noon on Monday I was struck by displacement... A person gets displacement as he gets asthma, and there is no cure for either' (ibid.: 4). Displacement and dislocations for Barghouti become here a clinical terminology, a periodic cycle of attacks which never leaves geography of the body. Displacement here is intertwined with both temporality and spatiality in the Palestinian context. For the ordinary Palestinians might get struck by displacement at any time: at noon, morning or evening, or at night. The relation of 'I' to the displacement here connotes multiplicity. If 'I' am displaced at noon then there will be someone other than 'I' who is displaced at night or afternoon or in the morning. The multiplicity of the self is a displacement and exile for a vast majority of the Palestinians. Theodore Adorno captures displacement aptly in his autobiography, *Minima Moralia: Reflections from a Damaged Life.* Adorno views that the bombings of the cities, houses, concentration camps by the Nazis, is at the same time, pitfalls of modernity. The advance of destructive weapons as a result of the development of civilization by technological means has negated and annihilated the 'possibility of residence' in which the idea of 'the house is past' (Adorno 1978: 38).

Writing about his experience of deportation from Cairo and coming back to Cairo, Barghouti writes, 'each temporary return completed the other half of a sentence. For all displacement is a semi-sentence, a semi-everything' (Barghouti 2003: 74). *I Saw Ramallah* is a memoir of exile, displacement and dispossession of the Palestinians in myriad ways. Time is always moving as Barghouti is well aware of 'the problem of stitching two times together' (ibid.: 76) and he has no doubt that it's not possible. As Norbert Bugeja observes, 'the narrative of suture is clearly intended as a redemptive gesture or at least an effort that will, in the last instance remain constrained to memoirist's narrative and its readers' own interpretation' (Bugeja 2012: 73). Two times: a past and a present cannot be coalesced into one. Agreeing to the fact that two times cannot be stitched together, Barghouti interprets both time and space in terms of the secular Jewish thinking, unlike the Zionist interpretation of time and space which is linear and denies the multiplicities or the existence of other cultures. The colonization of Palestine and the 'ethnic cleansing' which continues to this day with brutal repetitions by Israeli forces through war, building of settlements, zoning, checkpoints, bulldozing houses, and other means of creating 'facts on the ground' leaves the Palestinian people homeless, dispossessed, dislocated. Forced exile is a phenomenon which receives its legitimacy from the corridors of state power, both internal and external, renders living or dwelling a distant dream, a 'past' for the Palestinians in Adorno's sense of the word.

Barghouti's memoir places the reader right at the edge of a precipice; the reading subject opens itself to a text which does not take him to a precise point of a story or of a beginning. Barghouti fearfully approaches the Allenby Bridge on the Jordan River on his way to West Bank with skepticism whether he will be allowed in by Israeli authorities or his entry refused on flimsy grounds. As it is a daily routine at the Allenby Bridge where Israel holds the sovereignty of the both banks of the river, the Palestinians stand in queue, wait for hours until they get a clearance after scrutinizing of the papers, permits, passports and other documents by the authorities. Barghouti while crossing the bridge writes, 'A bridge no longer than a few meters of wood and thirty years of exile' (Barghouti 2003: 9). The bridge is a personification, as Norbert Bugeja observes, 'of the mental passage as he crosses into the territories with the memory of exile as his only return baggage' (Bugeja 2012: 60). Under 'Article X' of the first annex of the Oslo Accords of 1993, Israel retained the control of the West Bank-Jordan border. Eyal Weizman, the Israeli architect and geographer has dissected the Israeli plan of controlling the border in the name of security by dividing Palestine into Bantustans after the Oslo peace process. Weizman writes,

Article X describes in exhaustive detail a flow chart that separates the crossing into different color-coded lanes and sublanes, making up a complex choreography of trajectories and points of security checks that separate passengers according to the territorial definitions made in the Oslo Accords between different classifications of Palestinians separated by their place of registration: Gaza, East-Jerusalem, the West Bank under Israeli control (area C), the West Bank self-rule (areas A and B), and, finally, VIPs. According to Article X, incoming Palestinians would not see the Israeli security personnel who exercise overall control. Although present throughout the terminal/camp, that article provides that Israeli security agents would be "separated" from the passengers "by tinted glass." The travel documents of Palestinians crossing through the terminal/camp were themselves to "be checked by an Israeli officer who [would] also check their identity indirectly in an invisible manner." The Allenby Bridge spanning the Jordan River is the main connection between the West Bank and Jordan. There, Article X was implemented in the following manner: several interconnected rooms, partly glazed with one-way mirrors, were positioned at different intersections of the terminal's various pathways. Access to these rooms was provided by a back door. According to the article, incoming Palestinians would see only "a Palestinian policeman and a raised Palestinian flag" (also-as I saw at the terminal in 1999-an official framed portrait of Yassir Arafat against the background of the Dome of the Rock). A police counter stands in front of one of several one-way mirrors facing the "incoming passengers" hall. The mirrors are positioned so that Israeli security can observe not only the Palestinian travelers but also, significantly, the Palestinian police (Weizman 2006: 89-90).

The bridge is both a metaphor and the reality of existential conditions under which Israel exercises sovereignty and a small wooden bridge also acts as a wall of denial and access. Barghouti writes further, 'how was this piece of dark wood able to distance a whole nation from its dreams? To prevent entire generations from taking their coffee in homes that were theirs? How did it deliver us to all the patience and all that death? How was it able to scatter us among exiles, and tents, and political parties, and frightened whispers?' (Barghouti 2003: 9) The function of the bridge literally is to unite people across borders; a bridge is a passage of communications, happy unifications of families, uniting nations and cultures, exchange, transactions. For the Palestinians the bridge exists as if it doesn't exist. The bridge in its very presence and being, presents a history of absence of so many bodies that traverse it. Bridge is a chronicler of absence and presence par excellence. The bridge acts like a clock in Palestinian narratives of exile and displacement. When the bridge is not a bridge it is a wall or a fort or a trench or a deep chasm. Mahmoud Darwish's poem, *A Dense Fog over the Bridge* echoes the same feelings when he writes, 'my friend asked me, while the fog was dense/ over the bridge: Can a thing be known by its opposite?' (Darwish 2009: 160). The bridge here becomes a blockade to the passage, a barrier and a metaphor of exile. Barghouti writes further

> Here, on these prohibited wooden planks, I walk and chatter my whole life to myself. I chatter my life, without a sound, without a pause. Moving images appear and disappear without coherence, scenes from an untidy life, a memory that bangs backward and forward like a shuttle. Images shape themselves and resist the editing that would give them the final form. Their form is their chaos (Barghouti 2003:10).

There is a repetition at work here when Darwish evokes the same feelings about the bridge. As opposed to Barghouti's literary and metaphorical 'shuttle' (Reigeluth: 2008), Darwish employs 'dispersal' or 'schism'. Both Darwish and Barghouti are recognized in the contemporary world as prominent Palestinian intellectuals and poets and through their poetic and prose works gave voice to the Palestinian people in the cultural domain and literary world despite the blockade of Palestinian voices. Darwish wrote about the same Allenby Bridge, named after the British General who captured Jerusalem and later this very bridge was destroyed by Haganah, the Zionist forces in 1946 under the operation, 'Night of the Bridges'. Darwish writes,

> On the bridge I walk to my interior, tame myself,
> And attend to its matters. Each bridge is a schism,
> So neither are you as you were a while ago
> nor are the creatures' memories:
> I am two in one
> or am I
> one who is shrapnel in two?
> O bridge
> which of the two
> Dispersals am I? (Darwish 2009: 163)

The poetic works of Darwish and Barghouti 'complement each other chronologically by depicting pivotal eras of contemporary Palestinian history' (Reigeluth 2008: 294). Through 'diurnal repetition of being', Darwish and Barghouti, writes Reigeluth, 'perceive the endurance of existence.' In his introduction to Darwish's collection of poems, *If I were Another,* Fady Joudah suggests that in Darwish's poem, *A Dense Fog Over the Bridge,* 'self moves into its masculine other where fog competes with vision at dawn' and 'a dialectic' is at work where 'a thing cannot be known by its opposite'. Joudah writes further that 'the bridge has become iconic' for the Palestinian people as it is a symbol of steadfastness against horrific ordeals at checkpoints manned by Israeli security personnel. If the bridge evokes 'a memory that bangs backward and forward like a shuttle' for Barghouti then for Darwish, the bridge symbolizes 'schism' and 'dispersal' and for both of them the bridge becomes an existential agent of catastrophe for the Palestinian people. The bridge opens the wounds of Palestinians in exile, evokes a strong feeling of being exilic, dispossessed, scattered, and forces the Palestinian people to walk back into the memories of past. The presence of the bridge in the present tense of the word is a thread which connects the present with the past; the two times are coalesced in a metaphorical sense to become one.

Geography, Memory, and Repetition

In *Difference and Repetition* (2001), Gilles Deleuze formulates three different forms of repetition from the standpoint of the present. Deleuze's first synthesis is termed as 'passive synthesis' where lived present constitutes both the past and future dimensions of time. The past can be seen walking or journeying towards the future in the living present, 'thereby imparting direction to the arrow of time' where Deleuze argues, 'lived present constitutes a past and a future in time' (Deleuze 2001: 91). The second synthesis according to Deleuze is the 'active synthesis' of memory where memory swings between the two poles of time, the past and the present. Deleuze constitutes past in terms of the present as 'former present' and the present for Deleuze is always moving; he calls the contemporary dimension of time as the 'present present'. So memory can be seen oscillating between a 'former present' and the 'present present' according to Deleuze. Deleuze argues, 'memory is the fundamental synthesis of time which constitutes the being of the past' (ibid.: 101). 'Every present', writes Deleuze, 'passes in favour of a new present because the past is contemporaneous with itself as present' (ibid.: 103). In the third synthesis of 'empty time' the present becomes an 'agent', the past, a 'condition' for the future dimensions of time as Deleuze would suggest. It is Deleuze's second synthesis of memory which explains the temporal and spatial effects of repetition in Barghouti's memoir, *I Saw Ramallah*.

In the context of the life of a Palestinian, geography, memory and repetition fuse with each other in indistinguishable ways. The Palestinian predicament between history and geography has been poetically captured by Mahmoud Darwish. Darwish writes in the context of the Palestinian dispossession, exile and dispersion, 'the geographical part of history is stronger than the historical part of geography 'and,' history cannot be reduced to a compensation for a lost geography' (Darwish 1999: 81). While referring to interiors and interior facets of Palestinian daily life, of daily chores, activities, displacements, deaths, blockades, Edward Said (1986: 275) writes, 'the oddness of these excesses, and asymmetries, their constitutively anti-aesthetic effect, their communicated insecurity seem to symbolize exile - exile from a place, from a past, from the actuality of a home. But there is yet another problem being expressed in this form of repetition'. Mourid Barghouti's memoir, *I Saw Ramallah,* recounts the tragedy of his own people who either fell victim to the Israeli apparatus of assassinations or died in battles, raids, snipers, shootings, bombings, and indiscriminate firing by Israeli soldiers. Palestinians as a people always live in a 'state of siege'. Barghouti's encounter with the Israeli soldier with his gun at the Allenby Bridge is not a singular event for the Palestinians. The Palestinians face the presence of the soldiers in their everyday lives. Each soldier at the checkpoint reminds the Palestinian of his dispossession, dispersal, dislocations. Barghouti goes into a time when he witnesses the presence of the soldier during his procedural inquiries at the checkpoint. Barghouti writes of the encounter:

> This soldier with the yarmulke is not vague. At least his gun is very shiny. His gun is my personal history. It is the history of my estrangement. His gun took from us the land of the poem and left us with the poem of the land. In his hand he holds the earth, and in our hands we hold the mirage (Barghouti 2003: 13).

The presence of the soldier with the gun is a reminder of catastrophe. The present which he witnesses and experiences takes him to a pure past of the memories of the expulsion from the land. Also while crossing the Allenby Bridge, Barghouti encounters the past in the present. Memories of the dead, the martyred and the funerals are encountered by Barghouti. The memories of the dead ones and those who were assassinated by Israel or the ones who died in mysterious circumstances come here as a repetition; one tragedy after another. While Barghouti is waiting in a small guard's room to get his clearance permit to enter Palestine, he revisits the horrors and catastrophe of the past. In the room he observes a poster of Masada hanging on the wall. After giving the appropriate description of the room, Barghouti sees the dead ones 'coming through the door one after the other' (ibid.: 15). The repetition here is in the form of a series of 'entrances' of the dead in his memory. One 'Enter' followed by another 'Enter'.

> The Dead do not knock on the door.
> *Enter* my grandmother [...].
> *Enter* my father [...].
> *Enter* Mounif [...].
> *Enter* Ghassan Kanafani [...].
> *Enter* Naji al-'Ali [...]
>
> Their faces swam around me as though they were icons of Andre Rublyev, glimmering in dark temples in the thirteenth century. The armed guard's room was not dark, neither was the emptiness outside his room... Abu Salma entered and so did Mu'in and Kamal, and with them the poetry of their hearts that were bigger than their papers. Mounif and Naji came back a second time, and a third, and tension once again filled the room. Faces, fantasies, voices appear and disappear (ibid.: 15-19).

Each appearance of the dead in Barghouti's memory is followed by a detailed portrait of their lives and his own experience of being connected to these lives. The presence of posters in the soldier's room for example takes him to the Palestinian writer and political activist Ghassan Kanafani's own room which was filled with 'poems of Neruda, the words of Cabral, Lenin's outstretched hand, and the vision of Fanon' (ibid.: 16). Ghassan Kanafani was assassinated in Beirut on 8th of July, 1972 by Israeli squads who planted a bomb in his car. Another prominent Palestinian intellectual and artist, Naji al-'Ali was assassinated in London, of whom Barghouti remembers when Naji al-'Ali gifted him a painting. The death of his own brother Mounif, in mysterious circumstances in Paris, who could not see Ramallah again in his life, coupled with the death of his grandmother and his father appear in Barghouti's memoir while waiting in the soldier's room. The repetition of the dead appear in Barghouti's memory as 'one long continuous wail', (ibid.: 17) one after the other is a 'scar' in Deleuzian sense. As Deleuze (2001: 98) argues, 'a scar is the sign not of a past wound but of "the present fact of having been wounded": we can say that it is the contemplation of the wound, that it contracts all the instants which separate us from it in a living present'. Barghouti's experience of facing the Israeli soldiers at the checkpoint and the predicament of going through the ordeals to enter in his own homeland allows memory to swing back and forth, trapped 'between two presents: the one which it has been and the one in relation to which it is past' (ibid: 101). The memory here for Deleuze is a bridge which links the 'former present' and the 'present present' which is contemporaneous with the past. Deleuze defines memory in terms of the contraction which is derived from the passive synthesis of habit. Habit in Deleuzian sense is composed of 'contractions, contemplations, pretentions, presumptions, satisfactions, fatigues' (ibid.: 100).

Memory for Deleuze is 'the fundamental synthesis of time' constituting within itself 'the being of the past' (ibid.: 101) and the active synthesis of memory for Deleuze is a 'reproduction of the former present and reflection of the present present' (ibid.: 101). Henri Lefebvre's social space as the 'locus of prohibitions' gives rise to Deleuzian repetition of bodies in time and space, as Lefebvre (1991: 201) argues that social space is not just the space of 'no' but also 'space of the body'. 'In siege', Darwish (2007: 161) writes, 'time becomes place' and 'place becomes time'. The Palestinians as a people are daily witnesses to the horrors of siege by the Israeli military occupation. The space and time are mutually intertwined in a tragic way. Death becomes repetitive in the times of occupation of the Palestinian space. The assassinations, the martyrs, the dead repeat in Darwish's poem *The State of Siege:*

> Our losses: from two martyrs to eight
> every day,
> and ten wounded
> and twenty homes
> and fifty olive trees,
> in addition to the structural defect
> that will afflict the poem and the play and the incomplete painting (ibid.: 137)

Barghouti's narratives in *I Saw Ramallah* about the losses his people suffered as a consequence of defeat, colonization, assassinations, targeted killings, etc. take a repetitive turn again:

> This is not a personal matter that concerns me alone. Our catastrophes and our pains are repeated and proliferate day after day... An event descends upon its opposites and destroys in us all the anniversaries. Our calendars are broken, overlaid with pain, with bitter jokes and smell of extinction. There are numbers now that can never again be neutral: they will always mean one thing. Since the defeat of June 1967 it is not possible for me to see the number '67' without it being tied to that defeat (Barghouti 2003: 171).

Barghouti's memory goes back to Beirut days when the PLO began its second chapter of armed insurrection and guerilla fighting after its expulsion from Amman.

> Abu Tawfiq used to get into the jeep belonging to media services and drive around the streets of Fakihani in Beirut repeating the unchanging phrase "O our beautiful martyr!" He would then start to recount the virtues of the martyr we had just lost. At first the scene was moving. But the repetition of the falling of martyrs, the repetition of the funerals, the repetition of his favourite sentence, "O our beautiful martyr!" started to color the tragedy with a tint of routine familiarity, and into our day's sadness it would bring a strange kind of comedy... Mockery becomes one of the psychological tools that enable us to continue.
>
> Abu Tawfiq became accustomed to loss as the martyrs became accustomed to the repetition of their sacrifice, and as we who walked in their funerals became accustomed to seeing them off with the same slogans and noise to their metaphorical destination – Palestine – and their actual destination – the grave. The walls of Fakihani were covered with posters that bore their faces, but as more and more martyrs fell, the posters crowded each other on the walls, the newer faces covering parts of the older ones. Funerals were an integral part of the lives of the Palestinians wherever they were, in the homeland or in exile, in the days of their calm and the days of their Intifada, in the days of their wars and the days of their peace punctuated by massacres (ibid.: 176-177).

---

4. Reigeluth notes that the translator of *I Saw Ramallah* (2003), Ahdaf Soueif had to make several cuts to the original text in Arabic in order to minimize the literary repetition.

Stuart Reigeluth (2008: 307) notes that martyrdom in Beirut 'acquired new proportions', replete with massacres and the killings of the Palestinians[4]. The image of *Shahid* or martyr in the Palestinian context which occurs in Barghouti's first view is a tragic experience and when the same tragic appearance of martyrs in the form of repetition occurs then it becomes for him a comic scene. Deleuze (2001: 20) notes that the tragic and traumatic times can be experienced or lived 'only in the mode of repetition'. It is via 'repetition and co-occurrence within performative spaces,' states David A. McDonald, 'the image of *Shahid* has become a type of currency in the production of political and historical alterity' and 'cultural presence is substantiated by articulating the martyr in the form of repetition' (McDonald 2009: 79). Repetition as Deleuze (2001: 17) notes has two forms: the tragic and the comic, and 'indeed repetition always appears twice, once in tragic destiny and once in the comic aspect'. It is both the tragic and the comic aspect of repetition in *I Saw Ramallah* (2003) that paves the way for resistance in the form of *sumud* which also appears in Raja Shehadeh's memoirs as a way of resisting the Israeli colonization. Each repetition in Barghouti's memoir is caused by a difference, an absence in Deleuzian sense.

Barghouti (2003: 19) writes, 'the absent are so present- and so absent. This ennui surrounded by the salt of the Dead Sea... I am used to waiting.' Writing in relation to the Algerian resistance to French colonization, Frantz Fanon (2001: 194) wrote, 'comedy and farce disappear, or lose their attraction' but under the Israeli colonization of Palestine, the last remaining colony on the earth, 'comedy and farce' which was absent in Fanon's Algeria comes back.

Deir Ghassanah: 'Are We the Same at Parting and Meeting?'

Deir Ghassanah is the birthplace of Mourid Barghouti. Barghouti (2003: 56) asserts, 'here in this room I was born, four years before the birth of the state of Israel'; a powerful assertion of the lived experience against the farcical creation of the state of Israel born out of calculated myths and ethnic cleansing of Palestinians. This is a strong statement against the powerful design of Israel to get rid of all the Palestinians. Being born in a place is a beginning and an opening on to the world as beginning in the sense of coming into the world introduces, marks, the very place difficult to erase. Returning to Deir Ghassanah and his ancestral home after thirty years of exile, Barghouti's memory goes back to a time when his elder brother, Mounif was not allowed to enter Ramallah along with his mother. His brother Mounif had to part ways with his mother only to die a tragic death in exile, in Paris six months later. While entering Dar Ra'd, their old house, Barghouti writes:

> When I entered Deir Ghassanah his hand was in mine; we walked side by side to Dar R'ad, our old house. When I crossed the threshold for the first time in thirty years, the tremor that hit me was the same that took hold of me as I carried his body down into the grave on that dazed rainy day in a cemetery on the edge of Amman (ibid.: 36).

Entering the familiar landscape of his homeland and childhood days, Barghouti is hit by the 'tremor' of the loss of his brother. *I Saw Ramallah* is not a happy reunion of a poet and his homeland but a tragic entry after thirty years of exile and loss. Barghouti asks, 'Does a poet live in space or in time?' and then affirms, 'our homeland is the shape of the time we spent in it' (ibid.: 41). Unlike other intellectuals and political activists, Barghouti prefers a non-alignment with the political factions working in Palestine. He says, 'my measure is aesthetic' (ibid.: 43). It is through aesthetics of the daily life, Barghouti enters into politics. 'Where does this small lump in the throat and mind come from, while I am inside the dream itself? I have not exactly 'returned.' And so we return to politics' (ibid.: 43). 'In the Arab and specifically the Palestinian case,' notes Edward Said, 'aesthetics and politics are intertwined, for a number of reasons... One is the ever present repression and blockage of life, on every level, by the Israeli occupation, by the dispossession of an entire nation, and the sense that we are a nation of exiles' (Said and Barsamian 2003: 164). In *I Saw Ramallah,* aesthetics and politics intertwine rhythmically and periodically in the everyday lives of the Palestinian people. Barghouti laments that politics have been relegated to 'facts' or 'the eight O' clock news' against the daily aesthetics of people's 'emotions'. 'Politics,' writes Barghouti, 'is the family at breakfast. Who is there and who is absent and why. Who misses whom when the coffee is poured in the waiting cups... Politics is the number of coffee-cups on the table... Politics is nothing and it is everything' (Barghouti 2003: 43-44).

Upon entering Dar R'ad, Barghouti is surprised by another absence, the absence of the fig tree. 'I saw the fig tree—solid in my memory—absent from its place' (ibid.: 55). Deir Ghassanah is no longer a familiar place to the memoirist. This place too has been punctuated by dislocations, displacements and loss. Deir Ghassanah's loss which is Palestine's defeat is symbolized by the figure of Umm 'Adli whose son 'Adli was shot down by Israeli soldiers while trying to close the gates of Deir Ghassanah school at the heights of Intifada. 'Adli was the last hope for Umm 'Adli and she lived 'alone, with her face that carries the scar of an old burn, her peasant dress, her firm hands and green eyes, always sitting on the ground floor of the vast house' (ibid.: 59). Deleuze (2001: 98) notes that the 'scar is the sign not of a past wound but of a present fact of having been wounded'. 'The perpetuation of the ethnic cleansing of Palestine is carried forward through the allegorical body of Umm 'Adli, as the space of dwelling assumes corporeal features' (Bugeja 2012: 70).

Edward Said in his essay, *Interiors,* on the interior life of the Palestinian people through representations, remarks that 'these statements of presence' of the Palestinians in the occupied territories 'are fundamentally silent, but they occur with unmistakable force' (Said 1986: 280). This is the point where Bugeja observes that official historiography of Israel has failed in representing the Palestinian expulsion. It is Barghouti, observes Bugeja (2012: 71), who through his 'practice of memorialization' succeeds in furnishing 'a substitute for the official historiographical renditions of the occupied Palestinians' past'. Barghouti's presence in Deir Ghassanah after thirty years of exilic life spent in different corners of the world is punctuated by the lived experiences and images of the people he had left behind. One after the other Deir Ghassanah unfolds its painful stories to Barghouti. Just like the character, Funes, in Jorge Luis Borges' story, *Funes, His Memory,* while lying on the cot of his dark house 'could picture every crack in the wall, every molding of the precise houses that surround him' (Borges 2000: 98), Barghouti digs deep into the memories of his ancestral village and brings the dead, the martyred, the old, the young, trees, rocks, alleys, the guesthouse back into the present. The village guest house with all its people and peculiar smell is portrayed by Barghouti which brings back both space and time of the past in present.

> This, then, is the village square. This is the guesthouse of Deir Ghassanah, where the men meet every night to talk or condole or celebrate a wedding or receive a guest from the neighboring village or a far country. At once I smelled the scent of dark coffee and cardamom coming from the far end of the guesthouse wall where Yusuf al-Jabin pounded the coffee in the wooden mortar with a dancing rhythm. The square, the guesthouse, in front of me now and available to my five senses. Stone, not images—my eyes see it for the first time in thirty years. They stood up in front of me in their bodies, their clothes, their white headdresses, their faces. They stood up as though they had not died (Barghouti 2003: 68).

Memories are inscribed in space. Every space has its memories, stories and 'the past,' observes Lefebvre, and memory, 'leaves its traces; time has its own script. Yet this space is always, now and formerly, a *present* space, given as an immediate whole, complete with its associations and the connections in their actuality' (Lefebvre 1991: 37).

Prolonged occupation has pushed the Palestinians into a dependency. The underdevelopment of Palestine, erasure of the cultural life of its people, cities and villages is linked to the Israeli occupation of its land, resources and labour. Barghouti succinctly puts it in his memoir. The Israeli occupation has forced the Palestinians to remain 'with the old' (Barghouti 2003: 69). What Barghouti witnessed after his return to Ramallah after thirty years was that the city did not move forward but the underdevelopment of 'the past was still there, squatting in the sunshine in the village square, like a dog forgotten by its owners—or like a toy dog—I wanted to take hold of it, to kick it forward, to its coming days, to a better future, to tell it: "Run."' (ibid.: 70). As a result of the Israeli colonization, Sara Roy, a noted economist observes, 'the losses confronting Palestinians are profound, among them the potential collapse of the Palestinian economy and the impoverishment of virtually the entire Palestinian population' (Roy 2007: 251). The denial of the future to those who lag behind, notes Doreen Massey, is a projection of 'the singularity of the trajectory' and modernity's project of the 'temporal convening of geography' denies Barghouti's moving of 'past' into the future. This suppression of the marginal geographies by modernity's project of a linear time and space is what Massey (2005: 70) calls 'repression of the spatial'.

Writing and Resistance: Cartographies of Becoming

The Palestinians do realize the fact that the Zionist project of building a state only for its Jewish diaspora by excluding the Palestinians is a failed project. Upon his arrival in Palestine after thirty years of exile, Barghouti witnesses that 'the others are still the masters of the place' (Barghouti 2003: 38); there is no change even after the signing of the Oslo Accords. In their everyday lives Palestinians face the checkpoints, their identity cards checked, permits given and withdrawn, all at the mercy of the Israeli colonial practices. The Palestinians as a community and nation as Barghouti writes, are used to 'waiting'. The continued building of the illegal settlements doubled, especially after Oslo peace process as witnessed by Barghouti in *I Saw Ramallah*, adding another dimension to the internal displacement. The illegal settlements built by Israel as Barghouti writes, are not

> children's fortresses of Lego or Meccano. These are Israel itself; Israel, the idea and the ideology and the geography and the trick and the excuse. It is the place that is ours and that they have made theirs. The settlements are their book, their first form. They are our absence. The settlements are the Palestinian Diaspora itself (Barghouti 2003: 29-30).

Each settlement built in the occupied territories is conceived by Barghouti as the displacement of the Palestinian community. There is an inherent dialectics of presence/absence in the Barghouti's powerful statement. On the one hand, Barghouti sees the presence of the Palestinian diaspora in the ghostly architecture of the settlements themselves; on the other hand, he sees their absence which makes a very powerful claim between the presence of the absence and the absence of the presence. Bugeja (2012: 62) notes that the presence of the Palestinian diaspora and landscape is inherent in the space created by the Israeli colonial practices which have left a mark of Palestinian expulsion. The Palestinian landscape which has been transformed into an alien space by use of myths and machines by Israeli architecture, keeps the landscape from 'returning to nature,' and it is 'perhaps the general mode of presence or absence of the thing itself in pure language' (Derrida 2001: 4).

I Saw Ramallah is also a strange connection between displacement and writing. Barghouti conceives the idea of writing as displacement, a displacement from all sorts of power. Barghouti links his writing of exile and displacement to a cartographic practice much like Shehadeh does in his memoirs. For Shehadeh whose parents witnessed the al-Nakba of 1948 and displacement thereafter, writing became a tool to subdue the anger of displacement and dispossession. 'More than anything else,' writes Shehadeh, 'it was writing that was helping me overcome the anger that burns in the heart of most Palestinians' (Shehadeh 2008: 171). On a similar texture Barghouti writes,

> Writing is a displacement, a displacement from the normal social contract. A displacement from the habitual, the pattern, and the ready form. A displacement from the common roads of love and the common roads of enmity. A displacement from the believing nature of the political party. A displacement from the idea of unconditional support... If a person is touched by poetry or art or literature in general, his soul throngs with these displacements and cannot be cured by anything, not even the homeland (Barghouti 2003: 132-133).

For Shehadeh and Barghouti, writing in the form of memoirs became a strong tool against history's attempts at erasing the geography of their country's past, present and future. It is through their writings that they break the boundaries of displacement. Here writing attains a form, firmly rooted in defaced geography. As Adorno (1978: 87) states, 'for a man who no longer has a homeland, writing becomes a place to live.' Salman Rushdie too reaches a similar kind of conclusion about writing as Adorno does. Rushdie associates writing to a 'place' (Royle 2003: 45). In both Adorno and Rushdie, the conception of literature as a 'place' binds writing and literature to a certain kind of territorialization which gives a notion that literature is within limits. As Jacques Derrida notes, 'literature has no definitive meaning or resting place... The literary work never rests. Literature does not come home: it is strangely homeless, strangely free.' (Royle 2003: 45). The idea of literary work as 'displacement,' 'strangely homeless' opens up for a secular interpretation of culture and spatiality which in the Palestinian context challenges the whole idea of the exclusivity of the Jewish state. Also the idea of literary work along with its 'displaced' and 'homeless' character will be more free if it associates itself with the task of freedom, liberation, 'resistance' and the agency of 'becoming', away from all sorts of tyrannical practices of power and institutions in a Deleuzian and Derridean sense, rather than being a fugitive to the same. Barghouti's memoir, *I Saw Ramallah*, links these two ideas of literary work as 'displacement' and as well as 'resistance'. Barghouti for example questions the whole notion of boundaries, states and borders:

> Am I hungry for my own borders? I hate borders, boundaries, limits. The boundaries of the body, of writing, of behavior, of states. Do I really want boundaries for Palestine? Will they necessarily be better boundaries? ... No boundaries for the homeland. Now I want borders that later I will come to hate (Barghouti 2003: 38).

Gilles Deleuze in his essays on Foucault opens up a creative model for escape from the Foucaultian diagram and converts it into an event of escape thereby creating spaces for resistances in the form of 'becoming'. Deleuze writes,

> The history of forms, the archive, is doubled by an evolution of forces, the diagram. The forces appear in 'every relation from one point to another': a diagram is a map, or rather several superimposed maps. And from one diagram to the next, new maps are drawn. Thus there is no diagram that does not also include, besides the points which it connects up, certain relatively free or unbound points, points of creativity, change and resistance, and it is perhaps with these that we ought to begin in order to understand the whole picture. It is on the basis of the 'struggles' of each age, and the style of these struggles, that we can understand the succession of diagrams

> or the way in which they become linked up again above and beyond the discontinuities (Deleuze 1988: 44).

Deleuze turns this whole Foucaultian diagram into a map of multiplicities which opens up the avenues of 'free or unbound points, points of creativity, change and resistance' (ibid.: 44). Deleuze then turns out to change the whole diagrammatic practice of 'resistance and change' in the form of writing. Through cartography of writing Deleuze comes out with a triple definition of writing. 'To write,' Deleuze asserts, 'is to struggle and resist; to write is to become; to write is to draw a map' (ibid.: 44).

In *I Saw Ramallah,* Barghouti rewrites and challenges the dominant notions of spatiality in terms of a linear construction of cartographic designs like borders, checkpoints, walls, separate roads, etc.—both physical and cultural—by Israel for the exclusive Jewish state while pushing the Palestinians out. Barghouti's memoir then opens up a new cartography of Israel/Palestine space which allows it to be open and accessible to everyone. Barghouti demolishes the dominant assumption of the Israeli state by moving beyond the power politics which uses religion and religious texts to exclude and expel the Palestinians. Writing here becomes a force, a resistance, a space of creativity in Deleuzian sense which deterritorializes, smashes and builds up a new cartography of resistance in the form of writing memoirs. Writing is an act, a Palestinian way of resisting by staying put, not budging: steadfastness or *Sumud.* Shehadeh writes in his memoir, *Strangers in the House*, as he decides to write a letter to Kamal Boullata, a Palestinian writer living in the United States, 'I decided to write a letter to Kamal Boullata in which I would pour out the pain and frustration of my day, from morning until evening. I signed the letter Samed—the steadfast, the persevering...' (Shehadeh 2010: 146). Barghouti's memoir then becomes a force of Deleuzian 'becoming' in progression, opening up avenues for a secular interpretation of space, otherwise denied in official historiography of Israel and in its cultural production in the form of novels, memoirs, stories, movies, etc. Barghouti denounces that the Palestinians' quest for Palestine and their right to return to their homeland—unlike Israel—is not based on some sacred biblical myths and imaginations. Barghouti (2003: 7) writes, 'our song is not for some sacred thing of the past but for our current self-respect that is violated anew every day by Occupation.' Both Shehadeh and Barghouti's writing of memoirs brings another fact of writing which is linked to Deleuzian framework. The writings of both these writers become an act of *Sumud,* steadfastness. The Israeli siege on Palestine is unfolded and lifted in these memoirs in the form of writing as displacement, writing as steadfastness, writing as deterritorialization, creating a new cartography of resistance against the established cartographies of power and dominating structures. Fady Joudah, Darwish's translator observes that writing 'is a witness not only to human suffering but also to art under duress, art under transmutation' (Darwish 2007: xiv). For Darwish, writing is an act of resistance, ending the siege. So is the idea of writing for Mourid Barghouti. In Barghouti's poetics, Palestine multiplies. As Darwish Writes,

> I wrote twenty lines about love
> and imagined
> this siege
> has withdrawn twenty meters! ... (Darwish 2007: 151)

FOUR

POLITICS, ECONOMY, FICTION

We have nationalized God.

—Christian Gauss

We must think like a state.

—David Ben-Gurion

Imperialism and Zionism: Biblical Fantasies and 'Accumulation by Dispossession'

In his failed campaign to occupy Acre in 1799 resisted by Jezzar Pasha and his men, Napoleon in his strategic move appealed to the Arab and African Jews to rise in revolt against the Ottomans, promised the Jews of their 'return' to Palestine and reclaim their historic homeland (Kayyali 1977: 99). The French Journal *Moniteur Universel* on May 22, 1799 reported Bonaparte's proclamation inviting the Jews of Asia and Africa 'to come and gather under his banners to reestablish the ancient kingdom of Jerusalem[5]' (Schechter 2003: 201). West Asia

5. There are claims and counterclaims whether Napoleon issued such a proclamation or not. Historian Franz Kobler in his book, *Napoleon and the Jews* (1975) insists that Napoleon did issue such a proclamation for the restoration of Palestine as a homeland for the Jewish people. Simon Schwarzfuchs in his book *Napoleon, the Jews and the Sanhedrin* (1979: 25-27) argues that Kobler's source was 'forged' while maintaining that the story was 'created, and accepted in Europe, that many North African Jewish soldiers had joined Bonaparte's army' (quoted in Schechter 2003: 287) Amir R. Mufti agrees that proclamation was issued in *Moniteur* but there 'apparently is no text

and North Africa became a battleground for the French and British imperial rivalry. Searching for local allies along ethnic and religious lines, Britain invented the Jews as their ally in furthering their interests against French closeness to the practitioners of Catholic faith and Russian closeness to Orthodox Christians in the Levant (Sharif 1976; Kayyali 1977). In Palestine given its historical significance, Britain opened a consulate in 1839. Lord Palmerston, Foreign Secretary from 1831-1841, a key architect of the British imperial expansionism was among the early British Zionists to sow the seeds of a Jewish state in Palestine. On August 11, 1840, Lord Palmerston wrote a letter to the British Ambassador Ponsonby to call upon the Ottoman Sultan to open the gateway to Jewish settlement in Palestine as 'time is approaching when their nation is to return to Palestine' (Sharif 1976: 130). Palmerston shared the thoughts of Lord Shaftesbury who was praised in the *Times* newspaper dated August 17, 1840 for his statesmanship by upholding the cause of 'the Jewish people in the land of their fathers' (Sharif 1976: 130). Given the imperial rivalry between the French and Britain, Mohammad Ali's revolt in Egypt and challenge to the Ottoman Empire allowed Lord Palmerston to devise a strategy to counter the 'evil designs' of Mohammad Ali by floating the idea of Jewish immigration to Palestine. The revival of the biblical evangelicalism in Britain in the beginning of the nineteenth century and the expansionism of the British Empire connecting Egypt, Syria and Palestine to India guided Britain to establish a 'buffer state' with Jewish population in Palestine (Kayyali 1977; Sharif 1976). The British-Zionist connection was thus established advanced through

---

extant and the whole matter may be a hoax' (Mufti: 2007: 273). Philip Guedalla in his published lecture, *Napoleon and Palestine* (1925) writes that during his campaign of 1799, Napoleon became a 'momentary Zionist' (quoted in Millgram 1990: 43). Historian Salo W. Baron writes that Napoleon 'symbolized Europe's acknowledgement of Jewish rights in Palestine' (quoted in Millgram 1990: 42). Napoleon's proclamation is shrouded in mystery but it definitely created frenzy among Zionist historians and Napoleon was appropriated in the justification for the colonization of Palestine.

successive British Prime Ministers, military strategists and statesmen following the lines of Lord Palmerston. Along with the political and strategic drive of British Imperialism, the course of Zionist thought was taking shape in the literary and cultural sphere through the works prominent figures in the ranks of George Gordon Byron, George Eliot and Benjamin Disraeli. Various societies began to flourish giving shapes to colonization of Palestine and establishment of a 'Jewish State' (Kayyali 1977).

David Harvey observes that the inter-imperial rivalry and massive investments in trade and expansionism in the nineteenth century opening the way for colonization of the vast spaces of the earth ushered 'capitalist powers on the path of globalism' (Harvey 1990: 264). Spaces of the different parts of the world were 'deterritorialized' and 'reterritorialized' to suit the global imperial and colonial designs. In cultural realms, art and literature did not remain outside the fold of money-power relationships. 'Deterritorialization' and 'reterritorialization' or as Harvey calls it, 'time-space compression', was reflected in cultural realms where two times, the past and the present homogenized to form a single unity, as Harvey demonstrates, 'signals of a radical break of cultural sentiment that reflected a profound questioning of the meaning of space and place, of present, past and future, in a world of insecurity and rapidly expanding spatial horizons' (ibid.: 263). Marcel Proust's novel, *In Search of Lost Time* in seven volumes attempted to reproduce the past in the present to 'create a sense of individuality and place' (ibid.: 267). Proust's novel portrays the intertwining of time, memory and space with attendant tensions of modernism's architecture of building on the one hand and destruction on the other.

Zionism as a cultural product of the imperial and colonial mission unquestionably fit into the overall narratives of European representation. The representation of Zionism in literature especially in the works of British and the American literary producers like George

Eliot, Byron, Disraeli and others mentioned by Edward Said and Kayyali became a part of the cultures of European control and domination of the spaces of the *others.* The link between overseas colonial expansions was paralleled by the reframing of the space in cultural realm as Said's work in *Orientalism* and *Culture and Imperialism* proves.

The failure of European enlightenment in assimilating the Jews and the rise of anti-Semitism in Europe further strengthened the Jewish hope of establishing a state in Palestine. First the Dreyfus Affair in France and later the brutal Nazi repression and holocaust of the Jews was the product of modernity and enlightenment which produced in the words of Amir Mufti 'terrorized and terrifying figures of minority' (Mufti 2007: 2). Theodore Herzl, a Viennese journalist was covering the whole Dreyfus Affair. Zionism as a design grew up in the belly of Empire. Herzl wanted a Jewish State in Palestine. Said notes that the timing of Herzl's idea of colonial settlement came 'roughly at the same time as an antidote for anti-Semitism' (Said 1992: 70). Herzl's politics and his vision as Rodinson notes, 'unquestionably fit into the great movement of European expansion in the 19th century' (Rodinson 1973: 42). Herzl argued his case before the British Royal Commission (1902) for diverting the immigration of Jews to Palestine (Kayyali 1977). Herzl could not live to see the Zionist dream carried out by his successors. Chaim Weizmann, later to become Israel's first President, was close to the British diplomatic circles that in the end succeeded in procuring a favourable declaration from British Foreign Secretary Arthur J. Balfour on November 2, 1917 stating that Britain favours 'the establishment of a national home for the Jewish people'. The letter was addressed to Rothschild, a prominent Jewish businessman. Before the Balfour Declaration, the French and the British agreed to barter territories through the Sykes-Picot agreement in 1916 where Britain would keep Palestine, Transjordan and Iraq in exchange for the French interests in Lebanon and Syria. Weizmann was a prominent figure in the Manchester circle of Jews. Zionist historian John Kimche in his book, *The Unromantics* (1968) while cheering Weizmann's genius and diplomacy, openly flaunts the latter's British-Zionist connections. The timing of the book is perfect. It appeared to commemorate the celebration of 50th year of the Balfour Declaration. Kimche documents the shared interests of Britain and Zionism in securing Palestine for the Jews. He spoke with contempt towards Arabs— 'Arabs had no Weizmann' (Kimche 1968: 23). Britain and Zionism shared a give and take relation where Zionism had 'something to offer' and 'Zionists believed they were serving Britain's interests as much as their own' (ibid.: 29) in the course of Allied war strategy in West Asia.

In the course of the Balfour Declaration, Britain assisted Zionists in establishing Jewish institutions in Palestine, aiding settlements and other services at the cost of the Palestinians whose leadership was crushed by the British and never took a formidable shape. Lord Balfour himself was at the service of Zionism when he inaugurated the opening of the Hebrew University in 1925. Rashid Khalidi in his book, *The Iron Cage* (2010) captures the failure of the Palestinian people's struggle for attaining nationhood. Britain's handling of Palestinian resistance in a brutal manner was coupled with assistance to Zionists in creating a state power leading to the establishment of the state of Israel. Khalidi notes that the 'untiring efforts of the yishuv, the international Zionist movement, and Great Britain, which for at least two decades faithfully carried out its mandatory responsibilities to build up the Jewish national home, these institutions included, notably, a completely formed government bureaucracy and representative institutions, together with the core of a modern European-style regular army. By 1948, all had grown far beyond the embryonic stage, and indeed were fully ready to be born into independent statehood' (Khalidi 2010: 21). The Zionists got Palestine as an 'instant state' as the prominent geographer of Palestine, Salman Abu-Sitta describes the creation of the state of Israel. British cabinet headed by David Lloyd George as the Prime Minister who replaced Lord Asquith, appointed Herbert

Samuel, a prominent Zionist figure as the High Commissioner of Palestine in 1920. Earlier in 1915 Herbert Samuel drafted a secret memorandum titled, *The Future of Palestine: For the Use of the Cabinet* and sent it to the British cabinet suggesting that the Zionist cause can be served by 'the annexation of the country to the British Empire' and 'the country will be redeemed'. Samuel's memorandum turned out to be the basis for the Sykes-Picot agreement in 1916 which sealed Palestine's fate under the British Protectorate. In his letter to Lord Curzon, the Foreign Secretary Edmund Allenby, commander of the British Military wrote that Herbert Samuel's appointment as High Commissioner to Palestine was 'highly dangerous' (Kedourie 1969: 47). Once Samuel took his position as the High Commissioner of Palestine he went on to facilitate lands to the Jewish agencies through his various moves and tactics by bringing several new ordinances and laws, forming land commissions and surveys and by nullifying old laws established by the Ottomans.

As a result of the material, institutional and ideological support which was provided to the Zionists, they were able to expel and dispossess more than 750, 000 Palestinians, destroying more than 400 villages— a process of massive expulsion by force termed as 'ethnic cleansing' of the Palestinians by Ilan Pappé. The Palestinian Nakba or the Catastrophe is still entrenched in the memory of the Palestinians. By the time the British left Palestine and the establishment of the state of Israel was announced, Arab forces launched an all-out war against the Zionists. The Arab attack on Israel is termed by Zionists historiography and literary representation as a weak 'David' facing a marauding 'Goliath' hell bent on the destruction of Israel. Within no time the Zionist state managed to defeat the force of the combined Arab armies because of the massive strategy, gun-power, manpower which they built in assistance with the British colonial power successively. Isn't the declaration of a state on a land already lived, experienced and populated by the Palestinians an act of war? With the waning of British power and the rise of American imperialism, Zionism was not left in vacuum. The Americans replaced the British in their further expansionism and dispossession of the Palestinians. Within no time the American administration under Harry Truman recognized the state of Israel which was not only a symbolic gesture but a design for future mapping of West Asia where Israel will be their 'strategic' asset in the region. The United States' support to Israel as Noam Chomsky states is based on three aspects: diplomatic, material and ideological (Chomsky 2004). Chomsky clinically diagnoses the 'special relationship' between the United States and Israel in his book, *The Fateful Triangle: The United States, Israel and the Palestinians* (2004). During the 1982 invasion of Lebanon, Israel in an attempt to create a new map of the region supported by right wing Phalangist militias went on a genocidal project of aiding and killing of hundreds of Palestinians scattered in refugee camps in Lebanon. The massacre at Sabra and Shatila refugee camps by right wing Christian Phalangist militias supported and aided by Defense Minister, Ariel Sharon who was indicted by the Kahan Commission as 'indirectly responsible' was an eye opener for the entire world. Only the United States was blind to it. The United Nations Security Council resolution on June 26th, 1982 which called for a withdrawal of Israel from the Lebanese territory was vetoed by the United States. The same day the United States and Israel again voted against a General Assembly resolution calling for an end to hostilities which as Chomsky notes, was passed with two 'nays' and no abstentions. (ibid.: 9). These are the two examples of the U.S diplomatic power that allows Israel to act with impunity in regard to the Palestinians and the whole region. In the Veto list produced by the United Nations from the period 1946 to 2014 on the agenda items concerning 'Situations in the Middle East/Palestinian question/ Situations in the Occupied Territories', the United States stood alone by vetoing 40 resolutions in support of Israel, giving a green signal to act as 'Middle East Sparta in the service of American power', as

Chomsky (ibid.: 21) calls it[6]. On top of that, the United States' aid to Israel surpasses any limit. Chomsky notes that between 1978 and 1982, 'Israel received 48 % of all U.S. military aid and 35 % of all economic aid, worldwide' (ibid.: 10).

Israel is the only recipient of the U.S. aid which is excused from its accountability of how the aid should be used. Israel uses 25 per cent of aid budget to subsidize its own military industry 'which makes it virtually impossible to prevent the money from being used for purposes the US opposes, such as building settlements on the West Bank' (Mearsheimer and Walt 2006). The American [il]-liberalism goes well with Israel's policy of occupation, expansion, dispossession of the Palestinians from their own territories. 'The American liberalism', Chomsky notes, 'had always been highly sympathetic to Israel, but there was a noticeable positive shift in attitudes in 1967 with the demonstration of Israel's military might' (Chomsky 2004: 28). The victory of Israel in 1967 'induced open admiration and respect' among the American liberals and for others the same feelings were disguised in the form of myth created by Israel depicting a vulnerable 'David' attacked by hordes of 'Goliaths' (ibid.: 29). Chomsky sums up the U.S.-Israel 'special relationship':

> The historically unique U.S.-Israel alliance has been based on the perception that Israel is a "strategic asset", fulfilling U.S. goals in the region in tacit alliance with the Arab façade in the Gulf and other regional protectors of the family dictatorships, performing services elsewhere. Those who see Israel's future as an efficient Sparta, at permanent war with its enemies and surviving at the whim of the U.S., naturally want that relationship to continue (ibid.: xii).

---

6. See the United Nations veto list at http://www.un.org/depts/dhl/resguide/scact_veto_en.shtml.

The presence of a strong Israeli lobby, *American Israel Public Affairs Committee* (AIPAC) as a 'loose coalition of individuals and organizations' wields enormous power in the United States right from controlling and funding U.S. senators, members of the Congress, advocating regime changes in the region, managing propaganda in press, media, think tanks and other channels, and labelling dissenting voices as 'anti-Semite'. It's 'stranglehold on Congress' goes to the extent that 'some aspects of Israeli democracy are at odds with core American values'. The Lobby includes 'prominent Christian evangelicals' who share a common vision with the Israel of 'biblical prophecy' in support of its 'expansionist agenda'. The way the Israeli Lobby functions in pulling America towards Israel's maximalist goals undermining the core values of the United States is detrimental to the latter's own interests (Mearsheimer and Walt 2006).

1967 and After: Biblical Fantasies Continued...

The appeal to Biblical fantasies and imaginations coupled with the material practices of imperialism, gazing at the geographies of the *others* as 'empty' or as 'cultural barrenness' as Maxime Rodinson terms it, vocabularies that suited the missionary zeal of the colonizers is a common thread that links the three imperial powers. The French did it first, followed by the British and skilfully adapted by American imperialism—colonization is 'ostensibly seen as the spreading of progress' masking brutalities of power spread over non-European geographies (Rodinson 1973: 42).

The victory of Israel in 1967 termed as the 'triumph of the civilized' (Hirst 1977) in the western media, a victory of David against the 'bloodthirsty' Goliath paved the way for further colonization of Palestine. The colonization was justified on biblical grounds by the Israeli leaders. The war united all the political parties across the spectrum in Israel, from the left-liberals to the extreme right. The 1967 conquest and the consequent expansionism marked the creation of another set of Palestinian refugees. Israel achieved what it could not achieve in 1948. With the ideological backing and support of the West, the desire for *Eretz* Israel was nearly getting closer. The frenzy and the drive for more land had pushed Israel into madness. As David Hirst puts it:

> Like the Balfour Declaration and the 'war of independence' it created a whole new empty 'framework' to be filled in. Zionism has been reborn; their pre-war depression behind them, the modern Israelis rediscovered overnight something of the zeal and vision which had moved the early pioneers. It all gushed forth, this Zionist renewal, in a torrent of biblico-strategic, cleric-military antics and imagery. It was atheists talking about 'god of the armies'. It was paratroopers taking their oaths of allegiance, a bible in one hand and a rifle in the other, at the Wailing Wall. It was a spate of biblical poems and hymns set to jazz on the weekly hit parade. It was indefatigable parachuting warrior priest, Rabbi Shlomo Goren, resplendent in all his military decorations, planting the Israeli flag on the Mount Sinai. It was all, of course, at the expense of the Arabs (ibid.: 219).

In the Zionist imagination, 1967 was a return to a 'cosmic' and 'historical' time. It was not colonialism, but 'redemption' of the land lost in history. Overnight the Palestinians became refugees again. It was a strange twist of fate; time and history were not in their favour. The strange combination of Bible and the power of the gun dispossessed the Palestinians of their geography and culture. Israel issued an appeal to the Jewish Diaspora all over the world to come back to the land of David and settle while it was pushing the Palestinians out. The biblico-politico-military might of Israel combined with a messianic zeal of redemption of the land became an important tool for colonizing and accumulation of more lands and resources. 'The fierce contest over images and counter images' as Harvey argues, 'is an arena of action in which cultural politics of places, the political economy of their development and accumulation of a sense of social power in place fuse in indistinguishable ways' (Harvey 1996: 322). Israel as a nation was born in violence and 'ethnic cleansing' of the Palestinians. As Lefebvre argues, time and space are important sources of social power and the space is produced as a result of social and political actions over it.

Nationhood as Lefebvre argues implies 'violence'. The production of space is contingent on power; military, economic, social and political. In the case of Palestine the forces of discourse of knowledge and power created imaginary landscapes combined with the political-military-economic might of Israel. The Arabic names of the villages, towns and landscape were changed to invented Hebrew names. Judaization of Palestine was carried out since the beginning. 1967 accelerated the process of Judaization and changed the whole cultural landscape of Palestine. West Bank was consistently referred to as 'Judea and Samaria'. Trita Parsi (2007) observes that Begin was an important leader of the 'territorial school' who believed in holding as much land as possible since all of the lands belonged to the historical biblical kingdom. In fact, Menachem Begin's revisionist party *Gahal* was much more expansionist and racist in nature. It wanted 'no evacuation-even with peace' and would not even think of returning 'one inch of the land of Israel to any foreign government' (Hirst 1978: 220). The more territory it grabs, the more Jewish the state becomes. Shlomo Goren was one of the influential Rabbis of Israel. Just after the 1967 victory, Goren and company started a campaign about the conquered territories of West Bank by referring to them as 'Judea' and 'Samaria' underlining their messianic importance. Begin was quick to follow suit. Pappé writes,

> Goren and others began employing a messianic discourse about Judea, Samaria and 'Aza, areas presented as not only

> vital for Israel's survival but also for the advent of the Messiah. This eccentricity took centre-stage with the ascendance of Likud to power. Indeed, one of Menachem Begin's first acts was to instruct government personnel, including members of the media, to use biblical terms for the ccupied territories (Pappé 2010: 199-200).

The 'territorial school' was not a small one. It was ever expanding after the 1967 victory. From political leaders to right-wing Rabbis to settler common-sense, all of them spoke in the same language of territoriality. Moshe Dayan, the Defense Minister of Israel, too spoke in the same territorial expansionist terms. The Israel before 1967 for Dayan was not the real Israel as the vast landscape was still to be colonized. The journalist David Hirst captures the territorial essentialism at the core of the Israeli geopolitical thought. For Dayan, 'Old Jerusalem stood outside its frontiers and what was Israel without whole of Jerusalem? We thought that we had reached the summit, but it became clear to us that we were still on the way up the mountain. The summit was higher up' (Hirst 1977: 221) and knew no full stop for Dayan. There was no end to desire and territorial expansionism. While addressing the Kibbutz Youth Federation on the Golan Heights, Dayan said, 'There should be no Jew who says "that's enough", no one who says "we are nearing the end of the road" ... Your duty is not to stop; it is to keep your sword unsheathed, to have faith, to keep the flag flying. You must not call a halt – heaven forbid – and say that's all; up to here, up to Degania, to Mufallasim, to Nahal Oz! For that is not all' (ibid.: 221). Hirst notes, 'it was the apogee of the ideology of force' (ibid.: 222).

Israel was in full possession of East Jerusalem after the 1967 war. It started expelling the inhabitants living in this city for centuries by brute force. The Israeli forces bulldozed Arab houses, swept entire Arab villages. Hirst reports the destruction of the Palestinian villages thus:

> As they were driving bulldozers through the Maghribah quarters of Jerusalem, they were simultaneously wiping whole villages off the face of the earth. Among the first to go were Beit Nuba, Imwas and Yalu, situated close to the 1967 frontier in the strategic Latroun salient North of Jerusalem. Their 10,000 inhabitants were scattered to the four winds. In 1967 other villages such as Beit Marsam, Beir Awa, Habla and Jifliq, met a similar fate (ibid.: 228).

For many Palestinians 1967 was repetition of the 1948 al-Nakba as Hirst notes. Their return to Jerusalem after 1967 expulsion was made all the more impossible by the issuance of the Military Order No. 125 by the Israelis that prohibited any return of the repressed by punitive laws. Some Palestinians who tried returning back to what remained of their homes, at the dead end of the night by crossing the Jordan River were at the risk of being shot down by Israeli forces. Many Palestinians who were working abroad in Gulf States or were out for sometime during the war for business or academic purposes were outlawed by the Israeli authorities. Those returning without the permission from the Israeli authorities were termed as 'infiltrators' or had to face punishment for lifetime in Israeli prisons. The Israelis as Hirst notes, 'laid ambushes and shot everything that moved' (ibid.: 229). As in Jerusalem, the Palestinians who remained there were subjected to Israeli laws. They were new subjects under Israel without any political rights as are reserved for the Jews in Israel. Invoking a labyrinth of laws, Israel denied property rights to a majority of the Jerusalem inhabitants. The Land Acquisition for Public Purposes Ordinance of 1943, a British colonial law was brought into force to deny Palestinian their rights to land and property. 'The beauty of this law' as Hirst puts it, 'though not, of course, its framers intention— was that it could fit, such as turning Jerusalem into an emphatically Jewish city' (ibid.: 233).

Within twenty days after the June war, the unity government led by Levi Eshkol occupied 70 square kilometers of the land and incorporated around 69,000 of its inhabitants on June 27, 1967 (Weizman 2007: 25). Chaim Herzog, the first Military Governer of the occupied territories, later to become Israel's President took the responsibility of the destruction of the Maghribah (African) quarters as it stood just in front of the Wailing Wall. The whole lot of 125 houses was razed to the ground in no time. Herzog viewed this act as a 'historical opportunity' for Israel (ibid.: 38).

For the Palestinians it was a forced exodus on a massive scale. Some 200,000—one-fifth of the West Bank population—was forced to cross the Jordan River. As per Nur Masalha (2000), a Palestinian historian, nearly 300,000 Palestinians were forced to flee as a result of the Israel's gaining control over 90,000 square kilometers of territory as against the 20,000 square kilometers it held before the war. The war produced a 'territorial earthquake' in Masalha's view. His book *Imperial Israel and the Palestinians: The Politics of Expansion* (2000) dissects Israel's 'territorial maximalism' from 1967 to the present times. Masalha also shows how the transfer of the population as a result of the biblical frenzy created by 1967 war was openly discussed in the Israeli political circles from Labour Zionists to the extreme right across political streams. Masalha notes that post-1967 the Bible was brought again into the service by colonizing schemes of Israel. 'The influence of the Hebrew biblical narrative,' Masalha observes, 'in the secular intentions of Labour Zionism, particularly biblical conquests as narrated in the Book of Joshua, had always been evident (ibid.: 16). Biblical frenzy was not only a cry of the right wing Likud and Gush Emunim settler movements; Labour Zionism too was evoking the same sentiment among its people. Masalha argues that 1967 Israeli victory over Arabs altered

> Israel's geopolitical paradigm and cultural ecology. The war produced a spectacular territorial expansion. This territorial expansion made messianic religious and ultra-nationalist thinking seem highly credible. The 1967 conquests also

> made the historical Revisionist maximalist vision highly relevant. All the ingredients of Israel's new right radicalism– militarism, ultra-nationalism, territorial expansionism and neo-religiosity– produced political movements, including the new territorial maximalism of the Whole Land of Israel Movement and the fundamentalist settlement movement of Gush Emunim (ibid.: 22).

Few remained untouched by Israel's biblical mania of expansionism; poets, Rabbis, scholars, authors, university professors, right, left, centre, everyone was caught with this fever. Within the ranks of the Labour Zionism, 'The Whole Land of the Israel Movement' (*Hatnu'ah Lema'an Eretz Yisrael Hashlemah*) was born. Yitzhak Tabenkin was one of its prominent ideologues. Israeli Nobel laureate S. Y. Agnon was present in its foundational conference. The 1967 manifesto of WLIM declared that the new victory ushered Israel into a 'fateful period' and 'the whole of Eretz Israel is now in the hand of the Jewish people, and just as we are not allowed to give up the State of Israel, so we are ordered to keep what we received there ... ' (ibid.: 28-29). In the words of Masalha, WLIM 'laid the foundations of the project of imperial Israel' (ibid.: 28). Menachem Begin in whose name there are many recorded crimes was a non-compromising Zionist on the lines of Jabotinsky's 'Iron Wall' concept. Like Jabotinsky, Begin too claimed 'both banks of the Jordan River'. Begin was in favour of a total war to liberate both the banks of the Jordan and Gaza Strip since the very beginning. Begin argued in the Knesset in 1950 that West Bank was a part of the 'biblical land Israel'. Masalha notes that Begin argued against the superpower's call for Israel's withdrawal in 1956 Suez crisis. He insisted that peace in West Asia will be achieved 'only when both banks of the Jordan River and the Gaza Strip became part of the Jewish state' (ibid.: 68). At the fifth National Conference of the Herut in 1958, Begin evoking the slogan of the revisionist Zionist movement 'both banks of the Jordan – this one is ours and that one is also' called for a 'historic completeness' (*Shlemut Historit*) of Eretz Israel (ibid.: 68 & 73). Begin's Likud Party came into power in 1977. Begin changed the lexicography of the occupation. Against the Labour party's reference of the occupied territories as 'administered territories', Begin insisted on calling these territories 'liberated land' (ibid.: 73). Begin with his deputy Agriculture minister, Ariel Sharon who is referred to as 'the father of settlements' embarked on flooding the occupied territories of West Bank and the Gaza Strip with settlements which totally altered the physical and cultural landscape of occupied Palestine. Language was invented and employed to diminish the Palestinian presence, their culture, their geography and their history for the generations. The Palestinian poet, Mourid Barghouti aptly points out the politics of language in depriving the other of their space and history. Barghouti in his essay titled, *The Servants of War and their Language*, writes,

> The battle for language becomes the battle for land. The destruction of one leads to the destruction of the other. When Palestine disappears as a word, it disappears as a state, as a country and as a homeland. The name of Palestine itself had to vanish. The Israeli leaders, practicing their conviction that the whole land of Palestine belongs to them would concretize the myth and give my country yet another biblical name: Judea and Samaria, the fact remains that these territories are occupied (Barghouti 2003a).

Barghouti terms this colonial framing as 'verbicide'. Brutality is embedded in the language of Israeli colonization. The process of fencing, building settlements in the occupied territories of the West Bank and the Gaza Strip, separate roads for settlers, usurpation of natural resources like water, etc. has changed the entire landscape of Palestine. Ariel Sharon carried on Begin's policy ruthlessly. The destruction of Palestinian landscape by colonization is referred to as 'spaciocide' by Israeli sociologist Baruch Kimmerling. As Masalha argues, Likud under Begin and Sharon followed a *de facto* plan of 'creeping integration' enabling Israel to annex as much territory as possible from the Palestinians while resigning them to live in congested enclaves or Bantustans, a similar situation as the Blacks under Apartheid South African regime suffered (Masalha 2000: 77).

Palestine becomes a historic case of capitalistic 'accumulation by dispossession'. Expanding Marx's idea of accumulation and enclosures, the prominent Marxist geographer, David Harvey emphasizes that 'accumulation by dispossession' has become the hallmark of the latest phase of capitalism in the twenty-first century which he refers to as the 'new imperialism'. The 'organic relation between expanded reproduction on the one hand', as Harvey points out, 'and the often violent processes of dispossession on the other have shaped the historical geography of capitalism' (Harvey 2003: 141-142). If the new spaces are not available then capitalism must search an empty space for its perpetuation. The process of 'accumulation by dispossession' may take a variety of forms as Harvey suggests, depending upon the existing conditions. 'The commodification of cultural forms, histories, and intellectual creativity, corporatization and privatization of public assets', etc. as Harvey suggests are a new form of 'enclosing the commons' (ibid.: 148). The 'accumulation by dispossession' in Palestine takes the most subversive form of capitalist accumulation. The strange combination of force and biblical imagination is employed by the Zionist forces in occupying and dispossessing the Palestinians of their land, culture, story and history. In a different political context Mao said that power flows from the barrel of a gun but guns must not command the party. In the case of Israeli colonization of Palestine, it's the bible which wields power over the human psyche which holds the gun. The biblical imagination controls the gun and the psyche in the organization of the Jewish state. The Palestinians in the occupied territories are faced by economic hardships, not to mention the mental and physical abuse suffered at the hands of Israeli Defense Forces.

Creeping Apartheid and Pauperization

The Israeli colonial practice of 'creeping apartheid' as Oren Yiftachel calls it, amassing as much land and resources as possible minus the Palestinians have pushed the latter into a situation of dependency and 'pauperization' in the words of Palestinian economist Yusif Sayigh. Sayigh in his essay, *The Palestinian Economy Under Occupation: Dependency and Pauperization,* outlines two basic reasons for the underdevelopment of the Palestinian economy. One, the Palestinian economy of the Gaza Strip and the West Bank under Israeli occupation 'suffer from heavy, far-reaching, and debilitating dependence on the Israeli economy' and secondly, the Palestinian economy went through 'pauperization over the years' despite the Israeli claim of 'prosperity' (Sayigh 1986: 46). He argued that the classical dependency theory falls short in explaining the underdevelopment of the Palestinian economy as dependence is 'atypical' and the 'paradigm of dependency does not perfectly fit the case of the West Bank and Gaza Strip' as the Palestinians suffer from 'brutal dispossession' (ibid.: 52-53). Sayigh maintains that Israel does not allow the Palestinians to have a direct access to world market. As a result the manufacturing industry suffers heavy losses. The occupied territories become a 'captive market' and 'dumping ground' for Israeli goods. The unequal balance of trade is as astounding as Sayigh reflects that the West Bank and Gaza Strip imports 90 per cent of total imports from Israel constituting a single formation and economy (Sayigh 1986: 52-53; Farsakh 2013: 41). Sayigh dissects the bogus claim of 'inter-dependence' by Israeli economists. Israel extracts maximum profits through 'subcontracting arrangements, capitalizes on the fact that labor is cheaper in the occupied territories than in Israel and therefore is able to skim off more surplus value from the occupied economies as a result' (Sayigh 1986: 48). Post-1967 as Amira Hass, a distinguished Israeli journalist observes, 'Gaza Strip and the West Bank were subjected to an involuntary one-way customs union with

Israel: there was unrestricted commerce in one direction only—from Israel to the occupied territories' (Hass 1996: 135).

Labour becomes another source of 'structural deformation' as Sayigh maintains. The large scale land confiscations and water appropriation has forced a major chunk of Palestinian workforce out of agriculture, forcing them into vulnerability. By 1983 as Sayigh puts it, 87,800 workers from West Bank and Gaza Strip were officially employed in Israel constituting 37.8 per cent of the total work force. Moreover, the workforce employed in Israel is engaged in menial jobs and is considered by Sayigh to be of 'minor significance' for the Israeli economy. However, Sayigh underestimates the Palestinian workers contribution to the growth of the Israeli economy. The cheap labour provided by the Palestinians was 'one of the primary components in the massive economic boom Israel experienced throughout the 1970s and 1980s' (ibid.: 137). Thus even in this case there is no freedom for the Palestinians concerning the most important part of their lives: labour. There is no freedom of independent decision making when it comes to economy. The Palestinian economy is brutally tied to the chain of Israeli economy. Sayigh writes:

> The evidence shows that Israel has attempted with determination to tie the economies of the occupied territories to its own economy, and has largely succeeded... The exploitation of the occupied territories is effected by Israel as a whole-by its government, its capitalists, and labor alike. (The shades of difference between the behavior of Israeli management and labor marginally qualify, but do not invalidate, this statement.) Thus, the Palestinians have suffered external colonialism under the British, again at the hands of the pre-state Zionist movement, and now at the hands of the Israeli state as an occupier. Internal colonialism is much more destructive than external colonialism because

> it combines the uprooting, dispossession, and displacement of the national population with the imposition of a stunting dependency on the inhabitants who remain (Sayigh 1986: 52).

The 'pauperization' of the Palestinian economy is linked to the larger politics of the global political economy of capitalism. The relation of dependency as Sayigh argues is now 'sui generis' because of the larger capitalist structure of accumulation through its various 'tentacles of control' (ibid.: 53). The underdevelopment of Palestine and 'pauperization' of its economy is solely due to Israeli colonization of Palestine, Sayigh maintains unlike many economists who totally blame the Palestinians for their own predicament. As Leila Farsakh argues, 'mainstream economists rarely used the colonization framework of analysis when discussing the economic conditions in the West Bank and Gaza, Sayigh considered it key to explaining why the Palestinian economy could not develop' (Farsakh 2013: 43).

The Oslo peace process that was supposed to reduce the dependency of the Palestinian economy on Israel was an illusion. In her book, *Failing Peace: Gaza and the Palestinian-Israeli Conflict* (2007), Sara Roy exposes the false illusion of the Oslo peace process and through her research on the economy of the Gaza Strip, she came to the conclusion that Oslo further fractured Palestinian society, its unity and combined zeal to fight the occupation. Overall, the Palestinian economy went through a process of 'de-development'. In fact, Oslo did not at all lessen the Israeli grip on the Palestinian economy. Major questions concerning land, water, settlements, labour and capital were not resolved; sovereignty and borders were still controlled by Israel; military grip over Gaza Strip and West Bank remained intact. Roy thus contends that 'key structures of the occupation remained intact throughout the peace process' (Roy 2007: 81). Through the United States policy of aid, the status quo was maintained. United States never questioned the policies of Israeli occupation. The international community pledged $ 2.1 billion in assistance to the Palestinian community. The United States alone guaranteed 25 per cent of the aid. Despite the flow of aid, Roy observes that in the first three years of the peace process, 'socioeconomic conditions declined and the prospects for development reform dimmed despite the elimination of some key economic restrictions and massive infusion of foreign aid' (ibid.: 82). Thus aid became a tool of Israeli occupation and military control over Palestinian territories. PLO no longer was a revolutionary force. It became a vast bureaucratic structure dominated by Arafat and his cohorts. Oslo created massive resentment and opposition. Arafat's capitulation before Israel created massive anger and frustration in the Palestinian community. Oslo militarized the Palestinian society as Roy observes. More people were joining Palestinian Authority's security services as there were no options left to them. Nepotism ruled Palestinian Authority. Arafat's employment of senior Fatah members in the major sectors of the economy angered the Palestinians, Gazans in particular. Violence ruled the streets. PLO's capitulation before Israel and its waning popularity led to a virtual collapse of vision. In the absence of leadership and mass movement against the occupation, 'basic needs' superseded 'political activism' (ibid.: 84). Roy observes the crack within the Palestinian society:

> In a context so devoid of political and economic possibility, where power and bureaucracy, not philosophy, defined societal behavior, Palestinian resiliency eroded. This erosion was characterized by many features: a profound sense of betrayal among the people (regarding behavior of the Palestinian leadership); the continued receding of collective or participatory behavior (and the perceived importance of such behavior) in favor of the clan or tribe; the waning of community as an economic and social actor; growing inability to act (as opposed to react) other than through violence given

> the corruption and breakdown of institutional, political, legal, governmental and other kinds of channels, and the end, in effect, of a political or intellectual agenda within Palestinian society... By the end of the peace process—indeed, because of it—the social, economic, political and geographical terrain of Palestine had been dramatically altered and disfigured (ibid.: 85-86).

The 'pauperization' and dependency only heightened after Oslo. As Farsakh notes, the 'period between 2000 and 2012 was characterized by a clear case of Sayigh's pauperization, but at a much larger scale than what he reported in 1986' (Farsakh 2013: 46). Poverty in Gaza Strip touched up to 49.7 per cent and in West Bank this figure was 19 per cent (ibid.: 46). Farsakh notes, 'after 2000, the unemployment was over 20 per cent in the West Bank and between 33 and 45 per cent in Gaza' (ibid.: 46). The territorial split between Gaza and the West Bank after Israeli siege on Gaza in 2006 'aggravated the Palestinian economy's downturn' (ibid.: 46). Overall, the twenty years of the Oslo peace process has led to a 'declining income, not sustainable growth' (ibid.: 46). The separation of the Gaza Strip from the West Bank, the implementation of the closure, permit and checkpoint strategies only hardened Israel's grip over the Palestinian society and economy. As a response to the second *Intifada*, Israel invented the closure system for the first time only for it to become a permanent policy after the Gulf war, as Amira Hass mentions. Farsakh observes that Israel placed more than 604 checkpoints between 2002 and 2008 against 230 temporary checkpoints from 1993 to 1999. Checkpoints became a permanent feature after Oslo. There were 99 permanent checkpoints in 2012 along with an average of 310 flying checkpoints. Moreover, the 708 kilometers-long wall denies access to land to 11 percent of the Palestinian population— thus imposing enclosure on 250, 000 Palestinians. The closure of March 30, 1993 dealt a heavy blow to the Palestinian economy. As a result of the closure, Sara Roy observes that per capita GNP of the West Bank and the Gaza Strip combined fell by 30-35 per cent. Permits were denied to Palestinian workers to work in Israel. Out of the total workforce of 120, 000 in Gaza, only 56,000 had access to work in Israel, a sharp decline from a workforce of 80,000 before the Gulf War. Closure policy 'deepened Palestinian dependence on Israel over the long term, it has allowed Israel to begin restructuring economic relations with the occupied territories along new integrative lines' (Roy 2007: 112). Amira Hass reports a day in Gaza without work, closures imposed, permits denied, transports stalled:

> The heavy rain beat down on the workshop's roof and drummed against the windows. Every drop echoed in the big empty room where the sewing machines stood silent... Since early 1995 I had seen similar scenes over and over again—stilled factories that made cinder blocks or cosmetics, silent carpentry shops that once filed orders from the West Bank, a closed citrus-processing plant, a factory, that unable to ship the water containers it made to customers in other Arab countries, was left with one-tenth of its workers. In every place I saw the same empty chairs, the same couple of workers filing down some parts or greasing a machine, the same mounds of ready-to-ship products in a corner: cartons full of new telephone receivers, pretty floor tiles wrapped in plastic, empty cans gathering dust. For weeks or even months at a time, it is impossible to move goods out of the Strip; there is nowhere to sell them: not in Israel, not in the West Bank, not in Jordan, not in Egypt (Hass 1996: 287).

Israel had gained a monopoly over water resources. Water is another natural source through which Israel wields control. Most of the water from the occupied territories is diverted for settlers' use. Palestinian Authority has no control over its own water resources. Jacqueline Rose contends that 'Water will be politically crucial, a repeated stumbling block to peace—the Palestinian Authority has never been granted control of the water supplies. Today the settlements in the West Bank have seven times, and those in Gaza fourteen times the water supply of the Palestinians in refugee camps' (Rose 2005: 119). At the 1919 London Zionist Conference, Weizmann stated, 'I hope that the Jewish frontiers of Palestine will be as great as Jewish energy for getting Palestine. We must get all the waters which belong to Palestine to flow into Palestine' (quoted in Rose 2005: 120). In a memorandum submitted to British Labour Party in 1920 by the International Union of Labour Zionists, its draft prepared by David Ben-Gurion stated, 'It is necessary that the water sources, upon which the future of the Land depends, should not be outside the borders of the future Jewish homeland' (ibid.: 120). Water became another political instrument of occupation. On an average as Amira Hass states, the Palestinians in the occupied territories receive 93 litres of water per day (101 litres in Gaza and 85 litres in the West Bank) against the Israeli settler who receives 280 litres per day (Hass 1996: 145). Out of the estimated supply around 580 to 830 million cubic metres of annual water extracted from aquifers of the West Bank and Israel, the Palestinians consume between 110 and 133 million cubic litres in the region which constitute only 15-20 per cent of the supply. The rest is consumed by Jewish settlers and residents in Israel (ibid.: 146). As Elisha Efrat argues, the demand of the Palestinians that water falling on the zone of Palestinian territories should be consumed only by the Palestinians 'may cause great harm to Israel in two ways: it may worsen the sweet water and endanger the population's health in the central part of the country' (Efrat 2006: 66). However, Efrat does not mention about the harm to and health consequences for the Palestinians as a result of the bad quality of the water supply. The water supplied to the Palestinians has a foul smell. Hass reports of the constant headaches among Gazans as the chloride level in water exceeds 200 milligrams per litre (Hass 1996: 143-44). Efrat suggests that the water crisis in Gaza Strip can be solved by 'importing water from abroad' (Efrat 2006: 70). Efrat does recognize the unequal supply of water but her suggestion is clearly illogical. Why should water be imported by Gazans at their own cost while settlers in the occupied territories are privileged to have clean and uninterrupted supply of water? Israel's colonial racism is watery; its racism and exploitation runs across the topography like a free floating layer of liquid whose translucency hides beneath its crystal mask, a state running on sloppiness.

Along with the appropriation of water the building of settlements in the West Bank and the Gaza Strip in contravention of the International Law and the Geneva Conventions is practiced by Israel at a massive rate. Theodore Meron, a distinguished Jurist of international tribunals warned Israel in 1967 that 'civilian settlement in the administered [occupied] territories contravenes the explicit provisions of the Fourth Geneva Convention' (quoted in Chomsky 2010: 148). As of 2012, B'Tselem (2011), an Israeli human rights organization recorded 125 government sanctioned settlements, apart from 7 settlement enclaves in Hebron and 98 settlement outposts, 15 settlements in East Jerusalem. The Palestinians not only face spatial segregation in terms of house demolition, separation of roads, checkpoints, restriction on freedom of movement of the Palestinians, but also settler violence which acts as a para-state actor in occupied territories of the West Bank. The Israeli military which is supposed to protect the Palestinians from settler attacks in the occupied territories, in fact, shield these settlers. The justification of colonization in the form of building the settlements is done by a triangular process of biblical fantasies, Jewish messianism and legalization of illegal colonial occupation by setting up committees. Within Israel there are two narratives on the settlements which are opposed to each other. These narratives are a result of fear coupled with expansionist agenda. One narrative connects settlements to the core of

Zionism. In a commentary in *The Jerusalem Post* dated December 19, 2013, research scholar and historian Moshe Dan comments that the oppositions to the international law and the Geneva conventions 'strike at the heart of Zionism' as 'settlements are our Zionist marker in the sea of humanity' (Dan: 2013). The other narrative emanates from the fear of Israeli colonization of the occupied territories. It runs along the lines of Leo Tolstoy story, *How Much Land Does a Man Need?* whose major character Pahom, a greedy peasant in the quest of amassing more and more land could not reach Chief of the Bashkir's fur cap set as marker before the sunset and collapsed. 'If you try to grab it all, you end up with nothing', warns Ari Shavit in his article published by *Haaretz* on January 30, 2014. He went on to say that rather than the Arabs and the Palestinians being a threat to Zionism, Zionism is its own internal threat. 'Neither the Arab nation nor the Palestinian struggle threatens Zionism today, but the disastrous consequences of Jewish messianism do. The destruction sown in the West Bank has become a whirlwind endangering the Zionist dream more than any Arab storm' (Shavit 2014).

In a blatant move to legalize the illegal occupation, the Netanyahu government set up a three-member committee in 2012 headed by Edmund Levy, a former Israeli Supreme Court Justice and including retired Judge Tchia Shapira, the daughter of former Chief Rabbi Shlomo Goren, and attorney Alan Baker. The resulting 89 page report is yet another creation of 'facts on the ground'. The inclusion of Alan Baker as Chaim Levinson reported in *Haaretz* on January 31, 2012, casts a dark shadow as Baker 'was on the payroll of a settlers' organization advocating such legalization until nine days ago' (Levinson 2012). Levinson reports that Baker's law firm is involved in shady work which legalizes the illegal settlements and outposts.

> Baker's firm was recently hired by an organization working to legalize the outposts, which was set up by M K Uri Ariel (National Union) and Nachi Eyal, secretary general of Tekuma, one of the parties that ran jointly on the National Union slate. And just nine days ago, Baker and attorney Harel Arnon issued a legal opinion on the issue of abandoned property in the territories —an issue with direct bearing on Migron, one of the largest of the illegal outposts, which is currently slated for demolition on orders of the High Court of Justice. Migron is built on land registered to Palestinian owners. But the settlers claim that even if this registration is valid, the owners have left the West Bank and relocated to enemy countries, turning their land into "abandoned property" that ought to be managed by Israel's Civil Administration in the territories (ibid.).

The report is a cover up of illegal occupation and justifies the colonization of the West Bank which Israel held after the 1967 war as it argues that 'The classical laws of "occupation" as set out in the relevant international conventions cannot be considered applicable to the unique and sui generis historic and legal circumstances of Israel's presence in Judea and Samaria spanning over decades'. The Orwellian twist of the international law can be seen working when the report argues that 'according to international law, Israelis have the legal right to settle in Judea and Samaria' (Report quoted in Kershner: 2012). Israel's justification of the occupation by the Levy Report is that the West Bank was occupied because Jordan's sovereignty did not extend in the West Bank. The head of the International Committee of the Red Cross (ICRC) delegation for Israel and the occupied territories, Juan Pedro Schaerer in an article published in *Haaretz* on November

4, 2012, rebuked the Levy Report's partial and selective reading of a commentary published by the ICRC on the Fourth Geneva Convention for justifying the occupation. Schaerer cites the definition of an 'occupied territory' which is binding on the member states. Under the Hague Regulations of 1907 '[t]erritory is considered occupied when it is actually placed under the authority of the hostile army' (Schaerer 2012). 'Even the Israeli Supreme Court,' writes Scherer, 'has repeatedly and consistently ruled that the territory of the West Bank is subject to belligerent occupation' (ibid.). Schaerer concludes that 'contrary to what the Levy report maintains, from the viewpoint of international law the West Bank is occupied by Israel. This assertion, like the ICRC's position that the Israeli settlements in the West Bank are unlawful, is based entirely on the relevant provisions of international humanitarian law' (ibid.).

These are the 'pitfalls of national consciousness' embedded in the structure of colonialism, to use Frantz Fanon's phrase from *Wretched of the Earth.* For Palestinians, these 'pitfalls' of Israeli colonialism are a descent into the depths of a community's psyche. Fiction sets its own limit; realizing fiction in 'terms of creating 'facts on the ground' erases the very ground on which fiction's architecture is set. To end from where we began, Sara Roy notes that the sense of dejection, disillusionment and loss of dignity was felt as strongly as never before. Roy quotes a worker from Rafah refugee camp as saying: 'There's nothing left inside us. We are only shapes' (Roy 2007:95). A former member of the Popular Front for the Liberation of Palestine (PFLP) in Gaza echoes the same sentiment as the Rafah worker. He says, 'we have lost the political battle. Our expectations are low. Right now, we do not want a state; we want to get rid of the army so we can become human beings again. We are fed up with being nothing. We want our dignity' (Roy 2007: 95). As Mourid Barghouti sums up the occupation, 'the occupation forced us to remain with the old. That is its crime. It did not deprive us of the clay ovens of yesterday, but of the mystery of what we would invent tomorrow' (Barghouti 2003a: 69). The history of loss, dejection, dispersals, and dispossessions among the Palestinians can be felt in the words of Edward Said, 'every Palestinian represents concrete history of loss—of a society, a country, a national identity' (Said 1995: 46).

EPILOGUE

Zionism as a colonial ideology and discourse developed in context with overall European colonial expansionism and domination in the nineteenth century. As an ideology, Zionism shared the same ideas of space as did European imperialism in mathematical, Euclidean terms which means that a space beyond European territory is a 'container' or 'empty' devoid of social relations and stories of everyday lives linked with it. Alongwith the so called progress in science and technology, the *other* spaces were open for colonial exploitation, expansion of markets and domination of natives. The vast expansion of capitalism which took the shape of imperialism maximized profit as technology to a 'time-space compression' where vast spaces could be mapped in a short span of time with the development of railways, roadways, telegraph and other means of communication. The 'time-space compression' was also shaping the culture where colonies were represented in literary works. The idea of space as 'empty' outside the domain of Europe was also getting reflected in literary productions and discourses. Denying the multiplicities of space and lives and stories associated with space has produced a discourse at the cost of the natives spanning vast continents of Asia, Africa and Latin America. The geometrical 'emptiness' where imperialism unleashed its force for maximalist gains in accumulation of wealth and capital, coupled with the discourse of cultural and civilizational emptiness was used as a tool for colonial domination. In the Zionist imagination the conception of land acquired a subliminal state. The land of Palestine was imagined as empty, barren or poorly worked on by the natives in the Zionist imagination which, in turn, justified colonialism as Zionists claimed that they only can make the 'desert bloom'. The same discourse which established the state of Israel at the expense of violent expulsion and dispossession of Palestinians is carried out to this day. The narrative of Palestine as an 'empty' space despite being challenged and critiqued by Palestinian scholars, Edward Said foremost among them, is now used as a powerful weapon by the Israeli state to dispossess Palestinians and grab territory at a rate beyond imagination. The continuous production of the 'imaginative geography' is now used to justify the building of settlements in the occupied territories. The imperialist process of 'deterritorialization' and 'reterritorialization' of non-European spaces to create a capitalistic order also got reflected in cultural productions. Alongwith the British expansion and control of Palestine, a host of writers like Disraeli, George Eliot, and others were mapping Palestine in their literary writings.

Since 1967 Israel's use of bulldozers, forces, warplanes, and guns along with the 'imaginative geography' of Biblical imagination has dispossessed Palestinians for a second time. For Palestinians number signifies pain. Arithmetic is associated with pain as every attempt at the destruction of Palestinian community through waging wars repetitively is inscribed in Palestinian memory. Numbers signify continuous loss of people and territory. Territory becomes an object of desire and that desire can be fulfilled only by redeeming the land in the name of God and its book. The erasure of Palestinian spaces by reinventing Biblical names is another attempt at the destruction of Palestinian memory and landscape.

While addressing the Madrid peace conference in 1991, Yitzhak Shamir used the same tool of 'imaginative geography' invented by imperialism in 'pejorative' terms. Shamir cited a quotation from Mark

Twain's book, *The Innocents Abroad* which he wrote as a result of his journey to Palestine. The same colonial impulse still drives major literary and cultural productions within Israel. Amos Oz, a prominent Israeli novelist uses the same narrative of power and domination. His characters are inspired from reading *Moby Dick,* a novel written by Herman Melville at the time when American Empire was expanding and occupying the territories of Mexico by force. While Israel as a colonial power grabs more and more land, 'territorializes' by means of military and economic power, Oz as an apologist of the Zionist idea brings the same 'territorialization' in literature. The colonial construction and discourse have been challenged by Raja Shehadeh in his memoirs, especially in *Palestinian Walks: Notes on a Vanishing Landscape.* Shehadeh's writing decodes and deterritorializes the notion of Palestine as an 'empty' space that was politically constructed as a design. Another Palestinian literary figure and poet, Mourid Barghouti writes about a life lived in exile, his homeland out of bounds for him. Memoirs by Shehadeh and Barghouti while writing about their experiences of life 'deterritorialze' the Zionist 'geographical imagination'—former as a voice from the occupied territories and latter from the point of view of exile. Writing for them becomes a cartographic practice actually engaged in mapping Palestinian loss and dispossession. To write is to create, construct a map, engage in cartographies of resistance. In that sense writing becomes a revolutionary act in the state of siege. The Palestinians are resisting the Zionist colonization in various ways: *Sumud* (steadfastness), not moving away, writing about their experiences as in memoirs, novel, plays, etc and in oral tradition they have kept their hopes alive through a process of 'repetition' as Said calls it. Repetition by means of narratives and storytelling has become a means to resist colonization as repetition becomes a way of speaking, uttering and asserting 'truth to power', to use Edward Said's words. Repetition is stubbornness of memory, and of the child pointing out towards the wound—this is where it hurts.

The questions of fear and desire in the human psyche are grounded in space as combining the study of Lefebvre, Massey and Rose suggests. Israel by going back to the past in Biblical imagination is not only depriving a present and a future for the Palestinians but it is engaged in Borgesian 'circular ruins' where it is travelling on path of destruction as a nation itself. Both Palestinians and Israelis are caught up in each other's dreams. Israel thinks that as a state it is 'stable' but within the psychic geographies of the mind of its people there is an inherent fear and danger which is expressed in David Grossman's writings. Palestinians as a dispossessed and exiled community see themselves as victims of the victim which takes him to holocaust. In Shehadeh's writings, Jaqueline Rose suggests, pain does travel from one part of geography to another.

Spaces are never absolute or unending flat surfaces devoid of stories about people constantly in a flux. It is the moving quality of space, its dialectic, and its multiplicity that allows it to breathe freely. Identities are always moving, in a flux or flow. To deny the flow is to interrupt the social qualities of the space. A space constructed on racial purity is an end in itself. The establishment of Israel as 'Jewish state' grounded on racial, ethnic lines denies space not only to Palestinians but also to its Jewish citizens of Arab descent. In its inability to understand spaces, its contradictions, play of forces and emotions, memories inherent in the layers of spatial process, Zionism alongwith the attendant force of state and neoliberal capital seeks to homogenize space leading to *otherizations,* constituting a fundamental crisis of capital in spatial terms. Israel as a nation will always find it difficult to survive not only because of the subjective threats from without, but from the contradictions of the same space that it seeks to homogenize. Cohabitation, to use Hannah Arendt's word, multiplicity, recognition of the *other* is crucial in understanding the social and livable qualities of space. Suffering unless it is organized allows and opens the region for cohabitation. Edward Said's writings produces the contradictions

of geography and provides a way forward when he says in his text, *The End of the Peace Process: Oslo and After*, 'we cannot coexist as two communities of detached and uncommunicatingly separate suffering'.

BIBLIOGRAPHY

Abu El-Haj, Nadia (2001), *Facts on the ground: Archaeological Practice and the Territorial Self-Fashioning in Israeli Society*. Chicago: The University of Chicago Press.

Adorno, Theodore W. (1978), *Minima Moralia: Reflections on a Damaged Life*. London: Verso.

Arendt, Hannah (2007), *The Jewish Writings.* New York: Shocken Books.

Auerbach, Jerold S. (2013), 'Israel's Jewish Prime Minister', *The Jewish Press,* 13 September [Online]. http://www.jewishpress.com/indepth/opinions/israels-jewish-prime-minister/2013/09/13/ (Accessed 16 June 2014).

Audeh, Nabeel (1983), *The Third Way: A Journal of Life in the West Bank,* Raja Shehadeh, Reviewed in *Journal of Palestine Studies,* Vol. 12, No. 2, pp. 76-79.

Balaban, Avraham (1990), 'Language and Reality in the Prose of Amos Oz', *Modern Language Studies,* Vol. 20, No. 2, pp. 79-97.

Balibar, Etienne and Pierre Machery (1996), 'From Literature as an Ideological Form', in Rice and Patricia Waugh(eds.) Modern Literary Theory: A Reader. London: Arnold.

Barghouti, Mourid (2003), *I saw Ramallah*. New York: Anchor Books.

Barghouti, Mourid (2003a), 'Servants of War and Their Language', *Autodafe ¾: International Parliament of Writers*, New York: Seven Stories.

Barghouti, Mourid (2008), 'A Life in Writing', Interview by Maya Jaggi, *The Guardian*, 13 December[Online]. http://www.theguardian.com/books/2008/dec/13/mourid-barghouti.

Barghouti, Mourid (2011), *I Was Born There, I Was Born Here.* London: Bloomsbury.

Baron, Salo W. (1993), *A Social and Religious History of the Jews.* New York: Columbia University Press, in Millgram, Abraham Ezra(1990), *Jerusalem Curiosities.* Philadelphia: Jewish Publication Society.

Bove, Paul A. (ed.) (2000), *Edward Said and the Work of the Critic: Speaking Truth to Power.* Durham & London: Duke University Press.

Borges, Jorge Luis (2000), *Fictions.* London: Penguin.

Buber, Martin (1937), *I and Thou,* Translated by Ronald Gregor Smith, Available at http://en.bookfi.org/book/1078135.

Bugeja, Norbert (2012), *Postcolonial Memoirs in the Middle East.* New York: Routledge.

Butler, Judith (2007), 'I merely belong to them', (Review) *The Jewish Writings* by Hannah Arendt, in *London Review of Books,* Vol. 29 No. 9, 10 May, pp. 26-28, [Online]. http://www.lrb.co.uk/v29/n09/judith-butler/i-merely-belong-to-them.

Butler, Judith (2012), *Parting Ways: Jewishness and the Critique of Zionism.* New York: Columbia University Press.

Césaire, Amie (2010), *Discourse on Colonialism.* New Delhi: Aakar Books.

Chomsky, Noam (2004), *Fateful Triangle: The United States, Israel and the Palestinians.* New Delhi: India Research Press.

Chomsky, Noam (2010), *Hopes and Prospects.* Chicago: Haymarket Books.

Dan, Moshe (2013), 'Settlements and the future of Zionism', *The Jerusalem Post,* 19 December[Online]. http://www.jpost.com/Opinion/Columnists/Settlements-and-the-future-of-Zionism-335606.

Darwish, Mahmoud (1999), 'I Discovered that the Earth was Fragile and the Sea Light', *Boundary 2,* Vol. 26. No. 1. pp. 81-83.

Darwish, Mahmoud (2007), *The Butterfly's Burden* (Translated by Fady Joudah). Port Townsend: Copper Canyon Press.

Darwish Mahmoud (2009), *If I Were Another* (Translated by Fady Joudah) New York: Farrar, Straus and Giroux.

De Certeau, Michel (1984), *The Practice of Everyday Life.* Berkeley: University of California Press.

Deleuze, Gilles (1988), *Foucault.* Minneapolis: University of Minnesota Press.

Deleuze, Gilles (2001), *Difference and Repetition.* London: Bloomsburry.

Deleuze, GIlles and Félix Guattari (1983), *Anti-Oedipus: Capitalism and Schizophrenia.* Minneapolis: University of Minnesota Press.

Deleuze, Gilles, and Félix Guattari (1987), *A Thousand Plateaus: Capitalism and Schizophrenia.* Minneapolis: University of Minnesota Press.

Deleuze, Gilles and Félix Guattari (1986), *Kafka: Toward a Minor Literature?* (Translated by Dana Polan). Minneapolis: University of Minnesota Press.

Deleuze et al. (1998), 'The Indians of Palestine', *Discourse*, Vol. 20, No. 3, pp. 25-29.

Derrida, Jacques (2001), *Writing and Difference.* (Indian Reprint Edition 2012) London & New Delhi: Routledge.

Dosse, Francois (2010), *Gilles Deleuze and Felix Guattari: Intersecting Lives* (Translated by Deborah Glassman). New York: Columbia University Press.

Efrat, Elisha (2006), *The West Bank and the Gaza Strip: A Geography of Occupation and Disengagement.* New York: Routledge.

Ellis, Mark (1996), "Jerusalem and the Broken Middle: Reflections on Jews and Palestinians After Oslo', *The Arab Studies Journal,* Vol. 4, No. 2, pp. 133-148.

Fanon, Frantz (2001). *The Wretched of the Earth* (Translated by Constance Farrington). London: Penguin.

Farsakh, Leila (2013), 'Colonial Occupation and Development in the West Bank and Gaza: Understanding the Palestinian Economy through the Work of Yusif Sayigh', in Rochelle Davis and Mimi Kirk (eds.) *Palestine and the Palestinians in the 21st Century*. Bloomington: Indiana University Press.

Foucault, Michel (1980), 'Questions on Geography', in Colin Gordon (ed.) *Michel Foucault: Power/Knowledge: Selected Interviews and other Writings 1972-1977.* New York: Harvester Press.

Gonen, Arthur A. (1982), *Dissenter in Zion: From the Writings of Judah L. Magnes.* Cambridge: Harvard University Press.

Gregory, Derek (2004), *The Colonial Present: Afghanistan, Palestine, and Iraq*. Malden, MA: Blackwell.

Grossman, David (2006): 'Transcript of David Grossman's Speech at Rabin Memorial', *Jewish Journal,* 9 November, [Online]. http://jewishjournal.com/news/world/13973/.

Grumberg, Karen (2010), 'Of Sons and (M)others: Notes on the Spectropoetics of Exile in Autobiographical writing by Amos Oz and Albert Cohen', *Proof texts,* Vol. 30, No. 3, pp. 373-401.

Guedalla, Philip (1925), 'Napoleon and Palestine', in Millgram, Abraham Ezra (1990), *Jerusalem Curiosities.* Philadelphia: Jewish Publication Society.

Harvey, David (1990), *The Condition of Postmodernity.* Oxford: Blackwell.

Harvey, David (1996), *Justice, Nature, and the Geography of Difference.* Cambridge, Mass.: Blackwell Publishers.

Harvey, David (2003), *The New Imperialism.* Oxford , Oxford University Press.

Hass, Amira (1996), *Drinking the Sea at Gaza.* New York: Holt Paperbacks.

Herzl, Theodore (1989), *The Jewish State* (Translated by Sylvie D'Avigdor) [Online]. Available at www.mideastweb.org.

Hirst, David (1977), *The Gun and the Olive Branch: The Roots of Violence in the Middle East.* London: Faber and Faber.

Ilani, Ofri (2008), '1948 Diaries: Saving the Jews from themselves', *Haaretz,* May 5, [Online]. http://www.haaretz.com/print-edition/news/ 1948-diaries-saving-the-jews-from-themselves 1.245287.

Kaplan Eran (2007), Amos 'Oz's "A Tale of Love and Darkness" and the Sabra Myth', *Jewish Social Studies*, New Series, Vol. 14, No. 1, pp. 119-143.

Kayyali, Abdul-Wahab (1977), 'Zionism and Imperialism: Historical Origins', *Journal of Palestine Studies,* Vol. 6, No. 3, pp. 98-112.

Kedouri, Elie (1969), 'Sir Herbert Samuel and the Government of Palestine', *Middle Eastern Studies*, Vol. 5, No. 1, pp. 44-68.

Kern, Stephen (2003), *The Culture of Time & Space 1880-1918.* Massachusetts: Harvard University Press.

Kershner, Isabel (2012), 'Validate Settlements, Israeli Panel Suggests', *New York Times*, 9 [Online]. http://www.nytimes.com/2012/07/10/world/middleeast/israeli-panel-says-west-bank-presence-is-not-occupation-and-recommends-approval-of-jewish-settlements.html.

Khalidi, Rashid (2010), *The Iron Cage: The Story of the Palestinian Struggle for Statehood.* Oxford: One World.

Kimche, David (1968), *The Unromantics: Great Powers and the Balfour Declaration.* London: Weidenfield and Nicolson.

Kobler, Franz (1976), *Napoleon and the Jews.* New York: Schocken Books.

Lefebvre, Henri (1991),*The Production of Space.* Oxford, OX, UK: Blackwell.

Levinson, Chaim (2012), 'Lawyer who Worked for Outposts to sit on Israeli Government Panel to Legalize Them', *Haaretz*, 31 January [Online]. https://www.haaretz.com/lawyer-who-worked-for-outposts-to-sit-on-israeli-government-panel-to-legalize-them-1.410080.

Magnes, Judah (1930), 'Like all the Nations', *Jewish Daily Bulletin*, Vol. 7 (January 24) pp. 1-8.

Marx, Karl (1977), *The Eighteenth Brumaire of Louis Bonaparte.* Moscow: Progress.

Masalha, Nur (2000), *Imperial Israel and the Palestinians: The Politics of expansion.* London: Pluto Press.

Massad, Joseph A. (2006), *The Persistence of the Palestinian Question: Essays on Zionism and the Palestinians.* New York: Routledge.

Massey, Doreen (2005), *For Space.* London: SAGE.

Massey, Doreen (2008), 'Landscape/space/politics: An Essay', [Online], Available at http://thefutureoflandscape.wordpress.com/lands capespacepolitics-an-essay/.

McDonald, David A. (2009), 'Poetics and the Performance of Violence in Israel/Palestine', *Ethnomusicology*, Vol. 53, No. 1. pp. 58-85.

Mearsheimer, J. and S. Walt (2006), 'The Israeli Lobby', *London Review of Books,* Vol. 28 No. 6, 23 March 2006 pages 3-12, [Online]. http://www.lrb.co.uk/v28/n06/john-mearsheimer/the-israel-lobby (Accessed 17 July 2014).

Millgram, Abraham Ezra (1990), *Jerusalem Curiosities,* New York: The Jewish Publication Society.

Moore-Gilbert, B. J. (1997), *Postcolonial Theory: Contexts, Practices, Politics*. London: Verso.

Moore, Lindsey (2013), 'Ruins, Rifts and the Remainder: Palestinian Memoirs by Edward Said and Raja Shehadeh', *Postcolonial Studies*, Vol. 16(1), pp. 28-45.

Mufti, Amir R. (2007), *Enlightenment in the Colony: The Jewish Question and the Crisis of Postcolonial Culture.* New Jersey: Princeton University Press.

Negev, Eilat (2011), [Review Essay] *Hayyim Ketuvim (Written Lives: On Israeli Literary Autobiographies)* by Nitza Ben-Dov, *Haaretz,* 30 November [Online]. http://www.haaretz.com/misc/haa retzcomsmartphoneapp/the-thin-line-between-fiction-and-autobiography-in-israeli-novels-1.398727.

Nusseibeh, Sari and Anthony David (2007), *Once Upon a Country: A Palestinian Life.* New York: Picador.

Oz, Amos (1996), *Under this Blazing Light* (Translated by Nicholas De Lange). Cambridge: Canto.

Oz, Amos (1996a), 'The Art of Fiction No. 148', Interview by Shusha Guppy for The Paris Review, Fall 1996, No. 40. [Online]. http://www.theparisreview.org/interviews/1366/the-art-of-fiction-no-148-amos-oz.

Oz, Amos (2004), *A Tale of Love and Darkness* (Translated By Nicholas De Lange), London: Chatto and Windus.

Oz, Amos (2011), *My Michael.* London: Vintage.

Ilan Pappé (2006), *The Ethnic Cleansing of Palestine.* Oxford: Oneworld.

Ilan Pappé (2010), *A History of Modern Palestine.* Cambridge : Cambridge University Press.

Ilan Pappé (2014), *The Idea of Israel: A History of Power and Knowledge.* London: Verso.

Parsi, Trita (2007), *Treacherous Alliance: The Secret Dealings of Israel, Iran, and the United States*. New Haven: Yale UP.

Proust, Marcel (1992), *In Search of Lost Time* (Trans. Scott Moncrieff and Terence Kilmartin, rev. D. J. Enright 6 vols.). London: Chatto & Windus.

Ramakrishnan, A.K. (2014), 'Gandhi on Zionism and the Palestine Question', in Githa Hariharan (eds), *From India to Palestine*. New Delhi: Leftword.

Reigeluth, Stuart (2008), 'The Art of Repetition: The Poetic Prose of Mahmoud Darwish and Mourid Barghouti,' in Nassar H. and N. Rahman (eds) *Mahmoud Darwish: Exile's Poet.* Northampton, Mass.: Olive Branch Press.

Renfrew, Colin and Paul Bahn (1996), *Archaeology: Theories, Methods and Practice.* 1st ed. London: Thames and Hudson.

Rodinson, Maxime (1973), *Israel: A Colonial Settler State?* (Translated by Dacid Thorstad). New York: Monad Press.

Rose, Jacqueline (1996), *States of Fantasy*. Oxford: Clarendon Press.

Rose, Jacqueline (2004), [Review Essay] *Death as a Way of Life: Dispatches from Jerusalem, London Review of Books* Vol. 26 No. 6 18 March 2004, pp. 13-18. [Online]. http://www.lrb.co.uk/v26/n06/jacqueline-rose/failed-state.

Rose, Jacqueline (2005), *The Question of Zion*. New Jersey: Princeton University Press.

Rose, Jacqueline (2007), *The Last Resistance*. London: Verso.

Rose, Jacqueline (2008), 'Chroniclers of Pain', *The Guardian*, 10 May, Available at http://www.theguardian.com/books/2008/may/10/3.

Roy, Sara (2007), *Failing Peace: Gaza and the Palestinian-Israeli Conflict*. London: Pluto.

Royle, Nicholas (2003), *Jacques Derrida*. London: Routledge.

Said, Edward (1986), 'Interiors' in Mustafa Bayoumi and Andrew Rubin (eds.) *The Edward Said Reader*. New York: Vintage Books.

Said, Edward (1978), *Orientalism*. New York: Penguin.

Said, Edward (1992), *The Question of Palestine*. New York: Vintage Books.

Said, Edward (1993), *Culture and Imperialism*. New York: Knopf.

Said, Edward (1994), *The Politics of Dispossession: The Struggle for Palestinian Self-Determination, 1969-1994*. New York: Vintage.

Said, Edward (1996), *Representations of the Intellectual*. New York: Vintage.

Said, Edward (1999), *Out of Place: A Memoir*. New York: Knopf.

Said, Edward, (2000), 'Invention, Memory, and Place', *Critical Inquiry*, Vol. 26, No. 2, pp. 175-192.

Said, Edward and David Barsamian (2003), *Culture and Resistance*. Cambridge, Mass.: South End Press.

Sand, Shlomo (2010), *The Invention of the Jewish People* (Translated By Yael Lotan). London: Verso.

Sayigh, Yusif (1986), 'The Palestinian Economy under Occupation: Dependency and Pauperization', *Journal of Palestine Studies*, Vol. 15, No. 4, pp. 46-67.

Scott, James C. (1985), *Weapons of the Weak: Everyday Forms of Peasant Resistance*. New Haven: Yale University Press.

Sharif, Regina (1976), 'Christians for Zion, 1600-1919', *Journal of Palestine Studies*, Vol. 5, No. 3/4, pp. 123-141.

Shavit, Ari (2014), 'Settlements are Destroying Zionism', *Haaretz*, 30 January, [Online], http://www.haaretz.com/printedition/opinion/settlements-are-destroying-zionism-1.325310.

Schechter, Ronald (2003), *Obstinate Hebrews: Representation of Jews in France, 1715-1815*, Berkely and London: University of California Press.

Schaerer, Juan P. (2012), 'The Levy Report vs. International Law', *Haaretz,* 4 November [Online]. https://www.haaretz.com/opinion/the-levy-report-vs-international-law-1.474129.

Schwarzfuchs, Simon (1979, *Napoleon, the Jews, and the Sanhedrin*. London: Routledge & Kegan Paul.

Shehadeh, Raja (1982), *The Third Way*. London: Quartet Books

Shehadeh, Raja (2008), *Palestinian Walks*. 1st ed. London: Profile.

Shehadeh, Raja (2010), *A Rift in Time*. London: Profile Books.

Shehadeh, Raja (2010a), *Strangers in the House*. London: Profile Books.

Shohat, Ella (1988), 'Sephardim in Israel: Zionism from the Standpoint of Its Jewish Victims', *Social Text*, No. 19/20, pp. 1-35.

Shohat, Ella (1999), 'The Invention of the Mizrahim', *Journal of Palestine Studies*, Vol. 29, No. 1, pp. 5-20.

Shohat, Ella (2003), 'Rupture and Return: Zionist Discourse and the Study of Arab Jews', *Social Text,* No. 75, pp. 49-74.

Shohat, Ella (2006), 'Travelling 'Postcolonial', *Third Text*, 20:3-4, pp. 287-291

Shohat, Ella (2014), 'Columbus, Palestine and Arab Jews' in Parry et al. (eds) *Cultural Readings of Imperialism*: *Edward Said and the Gravity of History*. New Delhi: Aakar Books.

Soja, Edward W. (1989), *Postmodern Geographies: The Reassertion of Space in Critical Social Theory*. London: Verso.

Tolstoy, Leo (1993), *How Much Land Does a Man Need and other Stories.* London and New York: Penguin.

Twain, Mark (2010), *The Innocents Abroad.* London: Wordsworth Classics.

Yiftachel, Oren (2002), 'Territory as the Kernel of the Nation: Space, Time and Nationalism in Israel/Palestine', *Geopolitics*, Vol. 7, pp. 215-248.

Weizman, Eyal (2006), 'Seeing Through the Walls: Split Sovereign and the One-Way Mirror', *Grey Room,* No. 24, pp. 88-99.

Weizmann, Chaim, 'Zionist Policy' (address, September 21, 1919, London, British Zionist Federation), p. 18 cited in Jacqueline Rose (2005), *The Question of Zion.* Princeton and New Jersey: Princeton University Press.

Weizman, Eyal (2007), *Hollow land: Israel's Architecture of Occupation.* London: Verso.

Index